Intimate Coercion

Intimate Coercion

Recognition and Recovery

Marti Loring and Melissa Scardaville

ROWMAN & LITTLEFIELD
Lanham • Boulder • New York • London

Published by Rowman & Littlefield
A wholly owned subsidiary of The Rowman & Littlefield Publishing Group, Inc.
4501 Forbes Boulevard, Suite 200, Lanham, Maryland 20706
www.rowman.com

Unit A, Whitacre Mews, 26-34 Stannary Street, London SE11 4AB

British Library Cataloguing in Publication Information Available

Library of Congress Cataloging-in-Publication Data

Loring, Marti Tamm, author.
  Intimate coercion : recognition and recovery / Marti Loring and Melissa
Scardaville.
    p. ; cm.
  Includes bibliographical references and index.
  ISBN 978-1-4422-5432-9 (cloth : alk. paper) — ISBN 978-1-4422-5433-6
(electronic)
  I. Scardaville, Melissa, author. II. Title.
  [DNLM: 1. Coercion. 2. Family Relations. 3. Domestic Violence. 4. Family
Therapy—methods. HQ 515]
  RC569.5.F3
  616.85'8220651—dc23
                                                                2015014100

Printed in the United States of America

To all who have been—
or are now coerced—
may the light of knowledge
and understanding unlock
the cages of captivity.

Contents

Contents

Foreword

BY DAVID GRAND, PHD, DEVELOPER OF BRAINSPOTTING,
AND CYNTHIA SCHWARTZBERG, LCSW, INTEGRATIVE
THERAPIST AND CERTIFIED BRAINSPOTTING CONSULTANT

By carefully studying women's lives and their struggles, Judith Jordan, director of the Jean Baker Miller Training Institute at the Wellesley Center for Women, along with Marti Loring, director of the Center for Mental Health and Human Development, the Emotional Abuse Institute, have created new models of human development. These models focus on connection and the barriers/disruptions that can occur in connection, including violence and lack of empathy. Hopefully these models will help transform the destructive social impact of coercion as well as other societal ills such as racism, sexism, and classism. The practice of mutual empathy, which they promote, supports social justice and the belief that growth-fostering connections are central to human development.

Melissa Scardaville, presently working as a sociologist in health care, brings detailed research and literature to this book. She hopes that shedding more light on coercion will add understanding to the choices people make.

Marti Loring has worked with emotionally, physically, and sexually abused individuals for over thirty years. From this background she captures the lives of those who are ensnared by coercion. Her narrative illuminates, for both professionals and family/friends of such victims, an understanding of their profound challenges.

Loring and Scardaville hope this book will reach helpers of all kinds who could recognize coercion and emotional abuse, offering help and comfort to the trapped coerced persons, sometimes unable to see clearly what is happening in their lives.

Different from most books on an issue, this book not only gives examples but provides solutions and tools for therapists and others who intervene to help. The case studies bring home to the reader many actual experiences and dilemmas experienced during coercion.

The human stories in this book reflect the loss of self and the challenge to act against one's will. Those who are coerced are regularly threatened with harm to themselves, their children, and even pets. They have been shut out and isolated with almost nothing left but their intimate relationship and, as the authors have pointed out, leaving the relationship requires a functioning sense of self which coercion has taken away.

In many homes, the force of coercion is ripping apart the fabric of the family. Innocent victims are hurt, even killed, by plots hatched by those who are coercive. Intimate partner violence, coercion, sexual violence, and stalking are important and widespread public health problems in the United States. As this book suggests, violence deeply changes people: It alters the structure of lives, self-identity, self-esteem, and the ability to think and function with clarity and focus.

Women are by nature connectors. It is primarily within relationships that women grow and deepen their connection to self and others, and fostering connection is important to men and women from diverse backgrounds, so that the rupture of connection during coercion is both powerful and terrifying to the coerced individual, who fears during coercive threats for the safety of those dearest and most intimate.

As pointed out in this book, in a coercive relationship, the coerced person becomes increasingly isolated, more distant and disconnected from the other and themselves. Slowly a traumatic bond is developed and fear leads to greater fear, yet regret of loss, as well.

The healing process explained in this book can be as complex as the scars from coercion, and even more damaging than the physical injuries. The effects after the relationship has ended can be pervasive and long-lasting, and this is described by Loring and Scardaville.

People subjected to coercion are programmed into compliance and addressing the phenomena in therapy and other interventions is challenging. The therapist must be attuned to the subtle forms of emotional abuse and coercion experienced by those who are coerced. Loring outlines the eight essential components of the connective relational intervention model in working with the coerced, starting with the therapeutic stance marked by empathy and support, helping the fragmented self begin to integrate in connection with others.

Therapists are trained to diagnose in order to understand the client's experience and form a treatment strategy. However, for many coerced individuals, therapists can see struggles to keep alive . . . as manipulation, and can view profound anguish and sadness as depression, without understanding the forces causing these and other symptoms. It is essential for the therapist to validate the individual, develop a sense of trust, and perceive them beyond their individual behavior. Connection and caring, of the therapist and other community groups/causes, are crucial as the therapist supports the client's capacity for healing.

Loring and Scardaville have described various methods of therapy used in dealing with trauma, since coerced individuals are often profoundly traumatized. One of these methods that may be used prior to, or in conjunction with Loring's model for healing, is Brainspotting, an integrative model. It is a Dual Attunement model where the relational attunement is focused and framed by neurophysiological and somatic awareness to bring the client into homeostasis.

Brainspotting is based on the Uncertainty Principle where the therapist is aware of their limitations in witnessing the clients infinitely complex neurobiology. This principle places the choice and control back in the hands of the compliant individual and serves as an antidote to coercion. Although the client did not possess control over their partner's violence, they can discover their lost choice and self-awareness in the therapeutic relationship.

Loring and Scardaville, quick to point out others' valuable contributions to theory about coercion, depict the coercive process from the psychosocial perspective of forces that place a person (or group) in a stranglehold of impossible alternatives. Often law-abiding individuals are forced to participate in crimes that endanger others, forced in that terrible harm would come to themselves or loved ones (animal and human) if obedience does not follow threats and orders. Capturing the horror of coercion, Loring and Scardaville lay out the healing alternatives with the hope that therapists, others intervening, the justice system, and even the coerced individuals themselves, will grow in understanding this formidable process

Extending a plea to readers, Loring and Scardaville share their hopes, wishes, and aspirations that we will all reach out and join in an effort to protect adults, children, and animals caught in the iron grip of coercion.

Acknowledgments

ACKNOWLEDGMENTS FROM MARTI

Melissa, my coauthor and friend, shares a vision of hope for the coerced.

Thanks to family—for understanding and support—Esther Tamm, Don Devis, sisters Claire Blackwell, Joannie Walker, and Judy Tamm, Dr. Sid Tamm, Laurie Tamm, Phyllis Tamm, Dr. Irene Kaminsky, Bud Feuchtwanger, Elizabeth Picard, Tammy and Matt Dannheisser, and Reba Cockerspaniel.

Appreciation to supportive friends and professionals: Rev. Paula Buford, Mary Sinclair, Gillian Grable, Jacqueline Johnson, Marcia Ballard, Millie Williams, Susan Roseman, Harrell Warren, Anne Love, Dr. Jack Feldman, Chris Knox PA-C, Sherrie Eisman, and T. Bruce Nelson.

Kathy Steele took time to share her ideas about trauma and dissociation. And Dr. Gus Kaufman read through the manuscript at an early stage, contributing his ideas and suggestions, as did therapist Linda Weiskoff. Eager for their specialties to be understood by others, Dr. David Grand, therapist Cynthia Schwartzberg, Dr. Carolyn Rasche, and therapist Murray Dabby shared the richness of their treatments for those suffering from trauma. And our book grew from their sharing and assistance in writing clearly about each treatment.

We have all gained from those who have studied and written about intimate coercion: Thanks to Dr. Evan Stark, Dr. Judith Herman, Dr. Beth Richie, Dr. Mary Ann Dutton, and scholars/therapists from the Stone Center, such as Dr. Judith Jordan. And Dr. Bob Geffner has been an inspiration with his wonderful leadership and creation of trauma journals and books, as well as his vision for the future. Dr. Frank R. Ascione has studied and written about the plight of animals caught in abuse.

It's one thing to have ideas, and another to organize them into a book. I certainly appreciated the patience and guidance of Alison Pavan, Amy King, Kasey Beduhn, Meaghan White, Gary J. Hamel, and Suzanne Staszak-Silva at Rowman & Littlefield.

It was valuable to have had the opportunity to write an article with Dr. Pati Beaudoin and one with Tamara Bolden. Dr. Beaudoin has a deep understanding of abuse and coercion.

Thanks to Susan Wardell, Laura Switzer, and Sarah Heurich, wonderful mitigation specialists, and to caring investigator Dan Wells. Special gratitude to Greg Phillips, who taught me about coercion toward those with disabilities.

Many thanks to Erin Jansen, LCSW, and Kalie Lounds, LMSW, for wonderful adoption work at CHRIS Connections in Atlanta.

And heartfelt appreciation to Nora Sharp and her colleagues at A Family For Every Child, where they reach out to children across the country to find a "forever family": An adoptive home free from abuse and coercion. At the Women's Resource Center to End Domestic Violence in Decatur, Georgia, Kim Frndak and her colleagues share inspiration with women who dream of safe and happy lives. Sue Osthoff, director of the National Clearinghouse for the Defense of Battered Women, provides guidance to us in helping the coerced throughout our country. Many national animal organizations and local animal shelters find and care for those injured animals who have been victims of coercion, like Ahimsa House in Atlanta providing care for animals impacted by family violence, and much more. Any readers wishing to express appreciation for our book could contribute to these wonderful organizations.

I share both acknowledgment of their suffering, and profound hope that we will all reach out to protect animals who have become victims of coercers.

ACKNOWLEDGMENTS FROM MELISSA

I would like to thank my coauthor, Marti Loring, for the opportunity to collaborate and all the fellowship that followed. Thank you to the Rowman & Littlefield editors and to the professionals known and unknown whose insight and experience helped shape this into a better book. Thank you, too, to Darlene Deporto. Her class on domestic violence in the sociology department at Vassar College changed my way of thinking and brought a new passion to my life. Deep appreciation to Dr. Dina Zeckhausen and Dr. Brigitte Manteuffel for their thoughtful conversations over the years about trauma and for their support. Unending gratitude goes to my partner, Donna Bridges, who is the reason all this is possible.

Introduction

In "My Heart, Being Hungry" poet Edna St. Vincent Millay (1917) described the sometimes fruitless quest of feeding a hungry heart. This hunger can be emotional emptiness, where one longs for a nourishing love that affirms and supports the ideas, values, and qualities of another. With this love, a person's life journey can be less lonely and more fun, having a partner in the adventure of living.

Dr. Marti Loring, a social worker and sociologist, has seen how this hunger has affected her clients, people who have been coerced into acts they would have never committed on their own. Their hunger—born of sadness and loneliness—is fueled, not satiated, by their intimate relationships. For them, being loved is not an experience of support and encouragement; rather, they grieve over the loss of their own values and hopes, lost in the heartbreak of being used and exploited. For Dr. Melissa Scardaville, in her work with battered women and in research exploring various types of abuse, the patterns of coercion have been evident, although sometimes lost in the emphasis on various types and impacts of family violence. Both authors believe that people who are coerced with threats of harm or even death should not be judged in the same way as others who voluntarily participate in illegal activities.

Loring has conducted evaluations, written forensic reports, and testified in court settings for over thirty years. It is important to note that sometimes her evaluations do not indicate any coercion. Instead, there is willing participation in crime. All case study and therapeutic discussions presented in this book are based on her experiences. Research issues are explored by Scardaville, whose expertise is based on her sociology background, knowledge of research, and studies of various types of abuse.

During her career, Loring has evaluated hundreds of people. Some were not coerced, while others described experiences of coercion where they had been forced into unwanted behaviors that violated a cherished value system. Among those whose coercion ultimately led to illegal behavior, many express shock and surprise at their own actions. This surprise grows from the contrast between the person's normal behavior and values versus the coerced behavior. For example, Loring evaluated a gentle and kind woman whose husband threatened to kill her unless she participated in a bank robbery. Her husband waved a pistol during the robbery and frightened bank tellers. During the evaluation, this woman expressed sadness about the tellers' terror as well as horror that she was part of the robbery. Many coerced women exclaim, "I have never been in trouble with the law before—not even a speeding ticket!"

Feeling a sense of puzzlement, these coerced individuals trace steps of a life that strayed far from their plans, dreams, and hopes. Each needs help in finding where the way was lost, when goals disappeared, and how values were betrayed by some unwanted behavior that the person felt forced into. There is a sense of loss. The person's real self has been overshadowed or "disappeared" (like the lost people of South America who are kidnaped and disappeared from their families). Coerced women who have committed illegal acts feel disbelief and amazement at having been led into so much trouble by a loved and trusted intimate other.

In this book, the authors focus specifically on the process of coercion rather than attempting to review all aspects of intimate violence. Coerced women are called "the coerced" while coercive individuals are referred to as the "coercers." Different types of abuse are explored as they relate to the process of coercion. Emotional abuse is viewed as traumatic, either alone or with physical abuse (Loring, 1994). And emotional abuse is seen as occurring in an ongoing pattern rather than occasional slips of kindness that everyone commits when exhausted or frustrated. Overt emotional abuse can be very obvious—like seeing a friend's husband repeatedly calling her "stupid" and other derogatory names. However, emotional abuse can also be subtle, hidden, and covert, like ignoring a person's feelings, expressing disdain for an individual's career, or acting like someone's ideas are unimportant. Loring's exploration of emotional abuse led to her concerns about people who react to overt and covert emotional abuse, including threats, by obeying orders, some involving illegal behavior.

Loring has been consulted by many lawyers requesting an evaluation when they suspect a client may have been abused or perhaps forced into illegal behavior. These lawyers may have observed their clients exhibiting unusual behaviors such as fearfulness and unusually high anxiety. During her evaluations, Loring may review police reports, medical records of the woman and her partner, police department witness interviews, records of any past illegal behaviors by the woman and her partner, educational and work records of both, therapy records for both, and any other documents that would help understand them and their interactions. However, there are times when many of these documents are not available.

Loring also tries to interview others about the woman and her partner and how they seem to get along. These "collateral witnesses" can include family members, neighbors, teachers, coaches, church members, doctors, therapists, victims, and others who may have information about the situation. In some cases there are few collateral witnesses available. Further, she often uses tools to explore possible trauma symptoms, which will be discussed in this book. Abuse and coercion can lie at the heart of trauma, leading a woman to behave in ways that witnesses insist are not typical for her, even unusual or unbelievable.

A key to understanding and helping people is to see what the problem is: To accurately assess what's going on in someone's head and heart. The DSM-V is the diagnostic manual often used by mental health professionals to diagnose clusters of symptoms, to label groups of behaviors and characteristics of an individual, and to consider environmental stresses (American Psychiatric Association, 2013). The manual is used in forensic settings, such as court trials, to add understanding about an individual's life and behavior. One hope is that the case studies and analyses presented in this book will further an understanding and recognition of coercion that will be useful in diagnosis, treatment, and recovery.

In mitigation, the whole of a person's life is explored, from birth to the present. Their family influences are examined and trauma sources (if any) are identified. Educational history and health issues are discovered, as are other meaningful experiences. Mitigation can clarify behaviors that seem puzzling, out of character, and/or violent. An expert witness may be asked to explore this information about someone's life and testify to help others understand the person.

Other times, an expert evaluating an individual might share information gained in order to explain how the perception of impending harm or death can influence behavior. If an evaluation indicates there has been coercion, an expert could describe how the expected harm or death of the person or a loved one can lead to behavior intended to be defensive.

This book is not written by attorneys and will not delve into trial strategy or choices. Rather, the process of coercion and its impact on human beings is the focus. "Human beings" is a key concept, since coercion can be experienced by men and women, homosexuals and heterosexuals, Americans and those from other cultures, children and adults. However, feminine pronouns (*she, her*) will usually be used in this book in reference to the coerced since the majority of cases seen by Loring are women. A 2010 study conducted by the Centers for Disease Control and Prevention found that 41.1 percent of women had encountered some type of coercive control in their lifetimes, over 10 percent having an experience within twelve months of being surveyed.

The book also includes Loring's evaluations of other groups, such as children, adolescents, LGBT (lesbian, gay, bisexual, transgender) people, the disabled, partners of clergy, and the elderly. A chapter is devoted to these other groups with the hope of recognizing the existence of their suffering.

One goal of the book is to make the lives of the coerced come alive with clarity, to view their lives in a three-dimensional fashion; including all influences and experiences, the totality of joys and horrors experienced. Important is the sadness and impact of abuse—physical, emotional, sexual—and how these acts have pushed an individual to hope or hope-lessness, empathy or distrust, equanimity or rage, tendency to lead or certainty of following, ability to bounce back from adversity (resilience) or anguish and drowning in adverse circumstances. The authors hope that the coerced will be seen as whole people, including motivation and possible terror: Why did a person behave in certain ways when experienc-ing coercion?

That said, violent behavior is not minimized. The coercer and the coerced may leave many victims. Some have lost a lifetime of savings, including children's college funds and retirement investments, to phony investment schemes. Others have been traumatized during a robbery or bombing. And victims may suffer the heartbreak of experiencing injury or death of a loved one during violence planned by the coercer.

Recognizing the existence of powerful forces in someone's life can help answer questions that puzzle us. Why would someone behave in ways that are not consistent with her own values? Even though this behavior might not be illegal, it can be out of character and distressing for someone experiencing coercion. Other times, the coerced behavior can be illegal, whether or not the coerced is aware of the ultimate purpose of her tasks (this will be discussed later.) When there is a history of abuse and current trauma, it is important to piece together the puzzle of unusual or unchar-acteristic behaviors.

Many issues discussed in this book relate to coercion and impairment of functioning—either of the coercer or the coerced. There may be diag-noses by mental health professionals who have previously evaluated the coerced. Their pain and panic can lead to using alcohol and/or drugs to self-medicate and provide comfort during repeated traumatic experi-ences. A previous diagnosis of addiction, depression, or other condition should be acknowledged with an understanding of the interconnected impacts of abuse, coercion, and trauma. Otherwise, evaluating the abused and coerced may involve mislabeling. Symptoms of the abused must be viewed in the context of their coercion so that their attempts to avoid harm can be understood as such and their hopelessness, despair, and anguish do not appear to be depression alone.

Judith Herman attributed the problem of mislabeling to the following: "Concepts of personality organization developed under ordinary circumstances are applied to victims, without any understanding of the corrosion of personality that occurs under conditions of prolonged terror. Thus, patients who suffer from the complex aftereffects of chronic trauma still commonly risk being misdiagnosed as having personality disorders" (p. 117). Herman mentions "dependent" as a mislabel (p. 117). "Co-dependency" may often be applied to the coerced, although the damage to the self and fear of harm make independence hard to imagine until healing occurs in a safe environment.

In subsequent chapters, the case studies are disguised to protect the coerced, her family, friends, and employers. Understanding what the coerced experienced is vital in capturing the real meaning of coercion. Various theories and research about coercion are included in the book, as are different types of therapeutic interventions with traumatized individuals.

Coercion is a remarkable kind of suffering that often leads a person to:

1. Feel anguish and cut off from her own values and sense of hope
2. Despair about connection with a loved one
3. Experience a sense of horror about her own behaviors
4. Not recognize until later the full meaning of her participation
5. Feel terrified about harm to her, a loved other, and/or a beloved pet
6. Be systematically isolated from supports
7. Experience control in many behaviors
8. Hunger for intimacy with trust, respect, and deep caring

Chapter 1 is a brief overview of the academic research about coercion. The chapter is not comprehensive, and those whose interests lead to searching for more understanding about coercion would do well to explore the excellent works by Judith Herman (1997), Evan Stark (2007), Beth Richie (1996), Mary Ann Dutton and colleagues (2005, 2006), and Bessel van der Kolk (2014). Interested readers may find it valuable to review Dutton's theories on trauma in relationships, to see how Richie explored coercion from a cultural and gender perspective, to delve into Stark's philosophy and enlightening case examples, to discover Herman's insights regarding trauma treatment, and to understand van der Kolk's perspective on trauma and its physical consequences.

Chapter 2 includes information about therapy with the traumatized and/or abused. The coerced share both of these horrors, often having been traumatized *and* abused. This chapter outlines various types of therapy used to help heal trauma; the authors appreciate the kind help in writing this chapter from therapists who practice and/or have developed these methods. Included in this chapter is an important issue: Some of the traumatized may need help with their emotions before being treated. Trauma expert Kathy Steele explains that when feelings are overwhelming, it is important to have a stabilization phase prior to treating trauma. This preparation can include working on the regulation of emotions, like breathing and distractions (personal interview with Kathy Steele, February 9, 2015).

Chapters 3–7 involve an in-depth exploration into the dynamics of intimate coercion—from defining coercive mechanisms to recognizing distinct elements in the coercion process. These chapters are organized around theoretical aspects of coercion and illustrated by case studies that include the coercive events as well as the voices of the coerced.

Chapter 8 focuses on a sample of psychosocial evaluations done by Loring. In this chapter, each component of an evaluation is described and illustrated. The evaluations often contain a description of the individual's history—medical, family, counseling, psychiatric, army (or other branches of the service), and education. Past experiences and family relationships are highlighted. Additionally, there is an exploration of inner experiences (psycho) and external factors (social) that shape a person's vulnerability to coercion. Included in this approach are concepts such as self-esteem, resistance to coercive influences, resilience, and recovery from abuse. The interconnectedness of alcohol and/or drug addiction is noted: A coerced person may self-medicate using alcohol and drugs in her struggle to survive; at the same time, substance abuse often leads to escalating violence in an abusive coercer. As with the case studies, identifying information in the psychosocial evaluations is disguised. While some of the evaluations have been submitted to the court, others were used for different purposes, such as during plea bargain discussion by attorneys, or not at all.

Chapter 9 explores how coercion operates in other groups, including immigrants, people with disabilities, LGBT, church partners, children, adolescents, and elders. Readers can see how pain and suffering seeps through all of these groups when coercion dynamics confuse and traumatize the coerced.

Chapters 10 and 11 examine the transformation of the coerced. Transformative tools, including the language of acceptance and honoring, are described and discussed. For the coerced, transformation involves a growing wholeness that occurs along with an abatement of the haunting visions of coerced behavior. Many therapists combine trauma therapy, related in chapter 2, with some type of relational and supportive therapy, explained here. Loring shares connective relational therapy she has developed and used while helping the coerced to identify experiences of coercion, to regain confidence and a sense of their own identity, and to find self- forgiveness for coerced behavior that harmed others.

No doubt the question on some readers' minds remains: Why should we care *why* someone joined in some law-breaking behavior, like robbing a bank? Recognizing and understanding the existence of coercion makes a difference in our thinking: Was a woman threatened into driving the car that her husband used to rob a bank? What if he had harmed their son previously and insists that she drive his get-away car or he will kill their child? She could be a woman protecting her child and frightened that a bank teller might get hurt rather than a greedy bank robber who does not care if a teller is injured. And across America, many courts and laws honor the motivation for our acts. It matters whether one was forced to participate or actively volunteered for the experience.

Once we understand what drives the behavior, how we view that behavior—and any consequences it warrants—may change. Some of the coerced, overwhelmed with trauma, may not see the larger goals of the project that they have been coerced into joining. Often unaware of the hidden abuse, they do not understand their trauma, anguish, sadness, and confusion. They are driven, not by malice or evil intent, but by their hunger to connect with a loving partner who they once believed would encourage their growth into the self they dream of being.

1

Research Review

M any coerced people are very much prisoners of their own lives, held captive by those who used coercive control for manipulative and illegal ends. Sociologist Evan Stark (2007) observed that if we start by seeing the cage, then our understanding of coercion changes. Stark argued:

> The [domestic violence] literature documents violent acts and the harms they cause in agonizing detail. But this work suffers the fallacy of misplaced concreteness: no matter how many punches or injuries or instances of depression are catalogued, the cage remains invisible as long as we omit the strategic intelligence that complements these acts with structural constraints and organizes them into a pattern of oppression that gives them political meaning. (198)

We can see this in many of the case studies described in this book on coercion. Each act of abuse was a threat and a reminder that the coercer would harm, abandon, and/or kill the coerced if she stepped out of line. As soon as the manipulative acts were linked to one another, what were once isolated incidents became the bars of a cage. One hope of this book is that it will help people begin to see—or, if it is recognized, then put words to—that invisible cage of coercive control.

Over the years, researchers have worked to expose the cage of coercive control. Coercion was included in the power and control wheel, a framework about domestic violence (or intimate partner violence, IPV) developed by staff and by the battered women at a battered women's program in Duluth, Minnesota, in the mid-1980s. It defined coercion of a woman as: "making and/or carrying out threats to do something to hurt her;

threatening to leave her, commit suicide, or report her to welfare; making her drop charges; making her do illegal things" (Pence and Paymar, 1986). While some have criticized the framework for not adequately addressing social and psychological factors (Dutton and Starzomski, 1997), researchers generally agreed that coercion was related to power, control, and abuse. Ann Jones (1994) in her landmark book, *Next Time She'll Be Dead*, used Amnesty International's "Biderman's chart of coercion" to explain how men chose specific acts such as "isolation" and "deprivation" to control their intimate partners. From memoirs to newspaper headlines, the public has learned that physical violence is not the only form of domestic violence. All wounds are not visible.

In *Coercive Control*, Evan Stark deepened the way we think about coercion. Instead of saying that coercion was one of many ways that a controlling person could be violent, he argued that in coercive control, violence was one of many ways to control a person (2007, p. 242). In Stark's model, coercion, not violence, is both the context that gives meaning to everyday actions and the ultimate motive and endpoint. In his model, the yardstick that measures severity is not the number of punches or days spent in the hospital. Instead it is these little pinpricks of harm that add up over time. Each one by itself may not seem important, but together they create a web of entrapment. In this way, it is not just the acts—belittling, threats, isolation, and micromanaging—but their interconnectedness that becomes debilitating. An action that seems minor, strange, or even harmless now takes on a new more sinister meaning.

Stark's model of coercive control has four features: violence, intimidation, isolation, and control. These four features are tactical elements purposefully chosen based on what best undermines the woman. Violence is used in concert with intimidation and isolation. Violence may be physical and severe, but it is often "the frequency, relatively low-level, and cumulative effects of minor violence that distinguishes coercive control" (Stark, 2007, p. 243–44). Given the ever-present threat of violence, victims may feel like they can never relax or lower their guard.

Intimidation works in concert with violence by instilling fear, secrecy, and shame. Violence takes away a woman's sense of physical safety, while intimidation undermines her psychological power (Stark, 2007, p. 249). Intimidation can be threats against the woman herself or someone she holds dear, like a family member or close friend. The tool of intimidation helps to chip away at the woman's sense of self and any control she has over her own life. In intimidation, the perpetrator watches her every move, degrades her abilities, and/or humiliates her in front of others. The more frequent these acts of intimidation become, the more likely the woman is to see herself as incompetent and unworthy.

Isolation, a potent tool in the arsenal of coercive control, severs the woman's relationship to family, friends, neighbors, and coworkers. By keeping their partners apart from others, perpetrators are able to "prevent disclosure, instill dependence, express exclusive possession, monopolize their skills and resources, and keep them from getting help and support" (Stark, 2007, p. 262).

Finally, control is the tactic that directly allows the abusive partner to dominate the woman and dictate all the terms of the relationship. The one in control is the decision maker about every aspect of their lives, from routine activities such as when and how to eat, sleep, and have sex to access to lifesaving medical treatments for her and her children and/or pets. (Stark, 2007). Control is what keeps her captive in the cage.

Working together, the tools of violence, intimidation, isolation, and control not only trap women in the cage of coercive control but block any ways of escape. By outlining how these tools are systematic and interconnected, Stark showed how coercive control can change and slowly destroy the entirety of a woman's life.

Mary Ann Dutton and Lisa A. Goodman (2005) have also developed a framework in which we can better understand coercion. In their definition, coercion is composed of two pieces: a demand and a threat. They stress that coercive behavior can only be fully understood once the context of the behavior and the relationships are considered. They state that, "economic, political, cultural, familial, social, and individual factors—as well as their interactions—give meaning to an abuser's coercive behavior" (2005, p. 747). From this perspective, a coercive act becomes coercive in part because of who says it (and the amount of social power that person has) and in what context.

In the context of intimate partner violence, Dutton and Goodman argued that perpetrators must "set the stage" in order for coercion to be carried out in a relationship. They identified four factors that help create the conditions for coercion to take root:

1. Creating the expectancy for negative consequences
2. Creating or exploiting the partner's vulnerabilities
3. Wearing down the partner's resistance
4. Facilitating attachment (Dutton and Goodman, 2005, p. 748)

Each of these factors can be seen in the women's stories in this book. In every case, the coercer carried through on at least one threat to demonstrate that other harms—whether physical, sexual, emotional or financial—would likely happen if she did not comply with his demands. The abuser continued to set the stage by targeting areas in which the women felt insecure, such as parenting, intelligence, appearance, or social skills, assuring that they never gained confidence in these arenas. This repeated targeting depletes the women's emotional and psychological resources. The men also take away other resources—friends, family, sleep, money, careers—so that their partners have no way to counteract the barrage of fear and negativity in their home.

This book portrays the fearful and depleted state that wears down these women's resistance to the coercive control. Finally, through violence, isolation, and intimidation, the perpetrators force the women into dependency. These stories show how the women were left with almost nothing but their intimate relationship. In order to leave, one had to have a functioning self and coercive control took that away.

Dutton, Goodman, and their colleague R. James Schmidt continued this research by developing a way to measure nonviolent coercive control (2006). To that end, through much research and testing, they developed three interrelated scales that measured demands, threats of harm, and surveillance. Surveillance referred to behaviors of the perpetrator that were used to see if the demands issued were being followed. For instance, the researchers asked if the abuser had checked the woman's mail, clothing, receipts, car odometer, or bank statements, or had spied on, followed, or stalked the woman. They found that their measure specifically captured the coercion in intimate partner violence. Additionally, they developed questions that could guide therapists in discovering whether a client was experiencing coercion.

Beth Ritchie, in her book *Compelled to Crime*, also explored how coercive control destroys lives. Ritchie interviewed African American women who were in prison as the result of crimes they were forced to commit. She notes that multiple factors created the women's situation, including violence in their intimate relationships. She uses the gender-entrapment theoretical model to show four reasons that led the battered women she interviewed to engage in illegal activities (Ritchie, 1996, pp. 127–31). First, it was a response to violence (or threat of violence) or a way to postpone violence they knew they would experience at the hands of their partners. Second, the women felt loyalty to their partners and wanted to maintain stability in their relationship. Third, they believed the culturally constructed perception that it was their job as African American women to take care of African American males and the family as a unit. Finally, some women intentionally got caught in hopes that going to prison would protect them from future abuse.

Central to Ritchie's gender entrapment model are sociodemographic characteristics like gender, race, and class. Gender entrapment is "what happens to women who are marginalized in the public sphere because of their race/ethnicity, gender, and class and are then battered by their male partners. The model helps to show how some women are forced into crime by their culturally expected gender roles, the violence in their intimate relationships, and their social position in broader society" (Ritchie, 1996, p. 133). Ritchie also stressed the role of institutions such as the police or hospitals in gender entrapment. Many women in her study were ignored, shamed or mistreated by people who were in a position to help. Given all these factors, Ritchie argued that becoming involved in illegal activities was a survival strategy for many of these women. It was the only way to live in an almost unbearable life.

The stories that women tell clearly showed how intimate partner violence affected their sense of self. Marti Loring, in her book, *Emotional Abuse*, linked continued emotional abuse to the destruction of one's inner life. She defined emotional abuse as "an ongoing process where an individual systematically diminishes and destroys the inner self of another. The essential ideas, feelings, perceptions and personality characteristics of the victim are constantly belittled" (Loring, 1994, p. 1). This process, an essential part of coercion, complicates decision making for those being abused because their internal world is fragmented and disjointed.

Loring described overt and covert emotional abuse. People, including the victim, can see overt abuse, whereas in covert abuse, it is difficult for the victim and others to identify the patterns of discounts, negative labeling, negation, denial, projection, and disconnection. Those who are coerced are traumatized, isolated in sadness and fear. Depicting the terror experienced by these individuals who fear for their own lives and the lives of others, Loring identified the clinging and panic among the coerced women, who often only see their small part in an event, rather than the whole picture. To elucidate these situations, Loring drew on the work of Judith Jordan (2010) and scholarship from the Stone Center at Wellesley College, which offered a model of psychology for women that was relational and rooted in empathy. Discounting a woman's feelings coupled with violent threats toward her lead to a disconnection in the relationship.

Other scholars have applied alternative theories to explain how women are forced into illegal activities. Frequently discussed in the media is "Stockholm Syndrome." A criminologist and psychiatrist created the term "Stockholm Syndrome" in 1973 to explain why hostages during a bank robbery in Sweden emotionally bonded with and protected their captors. Underlying this concept is the idea of "traumatic bonding" (Dutton and Painter, 1981; 1993).Traumatic bonding occurs between individuals where a power imbalance exists and the one in control alternates between abusive and humane treatment of the other. Another related psychological concept is "learned helplessness" (Abramson, Seligman, and Teasdale, 1978). In learned helplessness, the victim feels that she is powerless so when the opportunity to escape arises, she believes any actions are fruitless. There is no point to resist, so why try?

Research in the areas of sexual coercion and stalking has explored prevalence of violence among intimate partners (Black et al., 2011). Over ten million women, an estimated 8.8 percent of all women in the United States, have been raped at least once in their lives by their intimate partner. Almost 1 million (0.08 percent) had been raped by their intimate partner in the last twelve months. Women also endured other types of sexual coercion. Over nineteen million U.S. women (15.8 percent) experienced some type of sexual violence other than rape by an intimate partner. Additionally, an estimated almost 11.2 million (9.2 percent) of women reported that they feared or were concerned about their safety because of stalking by an intimate partner.

Men, too, experience sexual and psychological violence. An estimated 10.8 million of U.S. men (9.5 percent) experienced some type of sexual violence other than rape by their intimate partners during their lifetimes, while an estimated five hundred thousand men (0.05 percent) reported being raped by an intimate partner at some point. An estimated 2.5 percent of men (2.8 million) indicated that they feared or were concerned about their safety because of stalking by an intimate partner.

While victims often believe they alone have suffered this abuse, studies such as these demonstrate that the coercive cage entraps many women, and some men, during their lives.

2

+

Treatment of the Traumatized and Abused

Bessel van der Kolk (2014) suggested that being traumatized means organizing life as if the previous trauma—unchanged and immutable—is still going on so that new experiences and relationships are contaminated by the past. For the traumatized, the past owns their bodies and continues to punish their muscles, moods, and sensations because of long-ago experiences. Van der Kolk also described traumatized individuals as overwhelmed with anxiety, dissociating and turning inward toward sensations and feelings from the past. According to van der Kolk, trauma brings feelings of abandonment and disconnection from the world. And the traumatized see themselves as unloved, empty, helpless, and trapped: Shut down and denying the source of trauma, those who are traumatized do not know how to be safe.

Van der Kolk found that trauma memories can be stored in disguised fashion; for example, the memory of helplessness experienced during a traumatic event can be stored as muscle tension. A rape victim who tried to push away her attacker may experience aching in her shoulder muscles, causing pain and distress. Van der Kolk described trauma as causing a rewiring of the amygdala in the brain so that past traumatic situations are interpreted as dangerous in the present.

What irony! Past experiences are causing grave discomfort, yet letting go of these memories and related sensations/anxiety involves their recall, which unleashes the terror that we strive to avoid. The challenge of healing involves learning how to help the traumatized to process and release buried feelings about these past horrors without being overwhelmed by their recall.

According to Herman (1997), there are different types of traumatic reactions. Some people can recover from a traumatic event and heal over time. Others experience circumscribed traumatic events, like a disaster, rape, or combat experience, which have formed the existing diagnostic criteria for posttraumatic stress disorder (PTSD). But the symptom picture is usually more complex among survivors of trauma that is ongoing. There are characteristic changes in personality among those who have survived prolonged abuse, including actual deformations of both relatedness and identity. Trust is damaged and connections with self and others are changed by trauma. Herman called this "complex post-traumatic stress disorder." Those experiencing this heightened trauma may have difficulty with traditional trauma therapy for PTSD. Kathy Steele and her colleagues, Suzette Boon and Onno van der Hart, pointed out that the trauma must not be worked on first. Instead, these traumatized individuals need a stabilization phase that supports learning more skills, including being more present and mindful, affect regulation strategies like breathing, distraction and acceptance of emotions as a normal part of life, and learning to tolerate discomfort a bit at a time.

When Dr. Paula Buford helps traumatized clients, she works carefully with them:

> When I work with persons who have been traumatized or abused, I am always mindful of keeping the relationship between myself and my clients as open and safe as possible. I do not want to replicate their abuse. I allow the client to set the pace for therapy and I am constantly reevaluating the relationship. Often, I give them choices of responding to me in writing and drawings, as well as verbally. Sometimes clients with PTSD have difficulty remembering our work from week to week. And during the sessions, they may seem foggy or spacey and may even be unable to move, hear, speak, or see. They are likely having a dissociative episode. My task is to help them to feel safe and grounded enough to be fully present in their bodies and present in the room. To bring them out of silence, I speak very slowly and gently. Then I help them to become aware of their bodies, like feeling their feet on the floor and other centering methods. (personal interview, Paula Buford, February 4, 2015)

THERAPEUTIC PRACTICES

A number of therapeutic practices have been used to help people struggling with the challenge of trauma. These interventions include mindfulness, tapping in/EFT (emotional freedom techniques), EMDR (eye movement desensitization and reprocessing), psychomotor therapy, neurofeedback, Brainspotting, Somatic Experiencing Therapy, cognitive behavioral therapy, dialectic behavior therapy, and the theater. A brief description of each follows.

Mindfulness

Ronald Siegel (2010) defined mindfulness as a practice and skill that involves "attuning us to our moment-to-moment experience" (p. 5). He advocates living in the present—right now—to experience whatever is happening in the moment. This can be difficult for the traumatized, since memories, sensations, feelings, and anxiety are overwhelming, cloaking the present with terrors from the past. Distressed by the flood of feelings, traumatized individuals may find it difficult to concentrate and focus during everyday life and therapy sessions.

Van der Kolk (2014) described "mindful self-observation" (p. 284). During therapy, parts of the self emerge from having protected the individual from trauma. It is useful for a therapist to stand back and observe what each part is protecting. For example, if a person avoided closeness with others because she felt worthless, it would be valuable to observe the self and get to know that part better, to identify how feeling worthless developed and how avoiding intimacy is involved in the current problem. Van der Kolk suggested that traumatized people need to observe the feelings and sensations in different parts of the body; the practice of yoga provides an opportunity for these observations (van der Kolk, 2014).

Anne Love is a psychotherapist who uses mindfulness techniques to help her clients develop an awareness of feelings and sensations in different parts of the body (A. Love, personal communications, October 22, 2014). Love explained that learning to accept and understand these feelings and sensations from the past is the beginning of a process. This process continues with letting go of the feelings and sensations in order to live in the present moment and be an authentic person: Mindfulness is a practice of awareness and letting go.

Mindfulness can be a tool for changing focus from past trauma memories and sensations to the present. And it gives people more choices for their own behavior when they can separate past fears and feelings from present hopes and actions.

Tapping In: EFT (Emotional Freedom Techniques)

The EFT of tapping was developed by Gary Craig (1995). EFT, borrowed from the Chinese, views the meridian system as energy circuits that run through the body. An individual tunes into issues while tapping meridian points on the body to stimulate them. When a distress memory is relived, causing disruption in the energy system, then tapping balances the energy system, letting internal calm replace negative emotions.

Tapping is a form of psychological acupressure. The same energy meridians are used as in traditional acupuncture. Tapping with the fingers inputs kinetic energy into meridians while the individual thinks about a specific problem. Also important are positive affirmations during the process, since negative thoughts can interfere with EFT working effectively.

Emotional affirmations, along with tapping the energy meridians, clear the emotional block from the bioenergy system of the body. This restores the mind/body balance, which is important for health and healing.

Eye Movement Desensitization and Reprocessing (EMDR)

Francine Shapiro (1995) has described EMDR as a process that can release long-held and frozen feelings and sensations that developed in response to trauma. Trained therapists help clients to target images and sensations associated with their trauma. Negative thoughts accompanying the trauma are also identified, like a belief that one is powerless—true during a traumatic event but a belief that can continue throughout life. Guided by a therapist, eye movement and other ways of involving both sides of the brain allow the traumatic experiences to be reprocessed. These eye movements help to release the feelings and sensations relating to the trauma. Once released, the emotions and sensations, as well as associated negative beliefs about oneself, lose intensity and can become truly in the past. These emotions, beliefs, and sensations can then be replaced by those that are informed by present experiences, such as moving from helplessness to power and choice in one's present life. The transition can include acquiring more positive thoughts and feelings, like shifting from negative thoughts about oneself to feeling a sense of mastery and self-management.

In her book, *Getting Past Your Past: Take Control of Your Life with Self-Help Techniques from EMDR Therapy*, Shapiro (2013) describes the automatic nature of responses that reflect past events, not the present experiences. Controlled by brain neurons outside of conscious awareness, a past belief—for example one believes that she is responsible for her parents' divorce—may continue to guide one's life in the present, without awareness or the opportunity to evaluate the truth of this childhood belief. Or a person can be held back in the present by a forgotten memory of being grabbed by her mother, held back and spanked while going down steps in quest of a ball. The child felt punished for reaching for something she wanted, a belief that continues to affect her adult life.

Shapiro suggests that if we remove a block, the body will heal. In her book, there are exercises that encourage people to remove the blocks themselves, although she reminds the reader that, if needed, therapy can help this process. Removing these blocks to freedom in the present involves reprocessing, which allows one to let go of past memories, beliefs, and sensations that block current functioning. Then reactions and responses in the present would no longer be automatic and driven by the past. Instead, past experiences would be digested and interpreted in a different way. Reprocessing these past experiences is key to EMDR.

Van der Kolk considers EMDR an effective tool to let go of the past for traumatized people. His research indicated that EMDR helps to integrate traumatic sensations and memories: "As our research showed, after EMDR people thought of the trauma as a coherent event in the past, instead of experiencing sensations and images divorced from any context" (2014, p. 255). According to van der Kolk, EMDR provided an opportunity to revisit the past trauma without causing additional trauma during the process (2014, p. 281).

Carolyn Rasche is a psychologist who is also an EMDR Institute facilitator and consultant approved by the Eye Movement Desensitization Reprocessing International Association. She views EMDR as effective in that it helps a client view a traumatic event as if watching a movie. Stepping back allows the brain to truly process the material (C. Rasche, personal interview, November 13, 2014). Previously the emotions and sensations would have taken over, as if the event is happening again. But using EMDR allows the cognitive side of the brain to work on the material, shifting away from negative beliefs. Using bilateral stimulation, she moves her hands back and forth as the client follows with her eyes, or taps the client on one hand and then the other, or uses bilateral sounds (like a beeping sound). Memories are processed and brought to a conclusion.

Psychomotor Therapy

Al and Diane Pesso developed psychomotor therapy to offer new experiences that help people overcome deficits in their lives (Pesso 1973; Pesso and Boyden-Pesso 2013). A person's history of not having her developmental needs met makes a difference when confronted with a traumatic event. These deficits create a vulnerability that leaves a person less able to cope with trauma. And, since trauma destroys a sense of meaning and hope in the world, a goal of therapy is to recover that meaning. In this intervention, a group is created and there are rules that allow an individual to feel safe in the group. The therapist and client figure out what basic needs were missed in the client's development and, together, they create a response that meets unfulfilled needs symbolically at the age when the response was needed and from the appropriate figures. Psychologist Gus Kaufman uses this intervention in his psychotherapy with clients. The task is to work with the client to understand the sought after response and create it. If a client is spaced out (dissociating), Kaufman might say, "That is an old response to trauma: What would you need to stop doing that?" The common response from a client who had not been protected during childhood would be, "Protection" (G. Kaufman, personal interview, November 13, 2014).

The therapist or someone in the group might stand in front of the client to protect him. And someone in the group might be picked by the therapist to play the role of a protective parent. The client and therapist discuss what would have been fulfilling as a child, like a parent acting in a protective, as opposed to an abusive, manner. Having agreed on the needs of the client, the therapist might instruct the group member playing the ideal parent to be reassuring. Thus, the client can tune in to unfinished business and feel at ease.

Kaufman might then say to this client, "Have you imprinted this so you can bring it up?" The goal is for the client to experience the missed reassurance from the past, and then remember the feelings of having experienced it in a safe setting. The hope is for the client to be able to recall and reexperience this fulfilling feeling afterward, gaining a greater protection from traumatic experiences and a sense of safety.

This treatment offers new and satisfying experiences for those with deficits in their development. The aim is to create feelings of meaning and fulfillment that allow more strengths such as joy and happiness to develop, thereby protecting against future trauma and adversity in life.

Neurofeedback

Another intervention some use to make changes in traumatized individuals is neurofeedback, which, according to van der Kolk (2014), can help change brain patterns. Trauma causes excessive activity in the right temporal lobe, the fear center of the brain. When people view a pattern of electrical activity in their brains, they can move from self-blame for their own behaviors to learning about how the brain processes information and fear.

Neurofeedback, a specialty in the field of biofeedback, utilizes information from an electroencephalogram (EEG) to depict current patterns in the cortex (Yucha and Montgomery, 2008). An individual is helped to observe and modify patterns to optimize brain activity by training them to change physiological activity and improve health and performance (Yucha and Montgomery, 2008). Instruments are used to measure a variety of physiological processes. One example involves measuring skin conductance (sweat gland activity). Self-calming by physical or cognitive techniques tends to lower skin conductance, while negative emotions like anxiety or fear often raise it.

Biofeedback can be useful in treating anxiety disorders, such as phobias. The term *training* is often used in this field, rather than *treatment*, suggesting a more active role for the participant (Yucha and Montgomery, 2008). These participants are usually asked to do homework in which they practice the skills of altering physiological responses of the body.

Biofeedback has been applied to a wide range of problems, including individuals struggling with trauma, headaches, and hypertension (Yucha and Montgomery, 2008). A helpful review of training and research is contained in the Yucha and Montgomery monograph. For those who have experienced trauma with subsequent feelings of helplessness, hopelessness, and somatic (body) pain, this type of training can produce a sense of power and hopefulness, in addition to decreasing physical discomfort.

Brainspotting

Corrigan and Grand (2013) describe "Brainspotting" as a technique that encourages clients to discuss emotionally difficult experiences that are linked to a visual focus. For example, one location in someone's visual field might become linked with memories of an attacker's raised fist. This link leads to strong activation of the body while recalling the incident. David Grand, Founder and Developer of Brainspotting, explained that Brainspotting works by identifying, processing, and releasing core neurophysiological sources of emotional/body pain, trauma, dissociation, and a variety of other challenging symptoms. Brainspotting makes use of the natural phenomenon of "where you look affects how you feel" through its use of relevant eye positions (Corrigan and Grand, 2013, p. 3). Together, the therapist and client pair a fixed eye and body position to an unresolved issue.

Cynthia Schwartzberg, LCSW, a Brainspotting therapist, suggests, for example, that ""when a therapist works with a client who experienced rape, the client could recall an attacker's rageful face. A relevant eye position and body feeling would be paired with the memory" (C. Schwartzberg, personal communication, November 14, 2014).

Grand has developed three primary methods of locating relevant eye positions in a client's visual field to be activated around a trauma. First, the "Outside Window" observes reflexive responses in the eyes, face, or body while slowly tracking a pointer across the visual field. Blinking can be an alert that signifies activity in the brain. The second way is "Inside Window" where a client is guided horizontally and then vertically to find the eye position where the somatic activation is experienced most acutely. "Gazespotting," the third method, involves observing and using where the client intuitively gazes while talking about the trauma. After the therapist locates a Brainspot by moving a pointer to find the location, a client is guided to maintain the gaze there and uncritically observe the internal process, which Grand calls "focused mindfulness" (Corrigan and Grand, 2013).

The therapist maintains a nonthreatening gaze at the client, thereby helping the client to continue attentiveness to the body's feelings and sensations attached to the Brainspot. Giving the process as much time and repetition as needed is important "to rewrite the neural pathways that were previously entrenched in maladaptive and dysfunctional loops" (Corrigan and Grand, 2013, p.2).

Somatic Therapy

Somatic Experiencing Therapy was developed by Peter Levine. In essence, the energy caused by a trauma needs to be discharged. A threatening event puts the lower brain—the more primitive brain—on alert. Higher-level executive functions are less active in the face of these dominant lower-level neurological reactions: fight, flight, or freeze. In the animal kingdom (Levine originally studied wildlife) an animal releases the chemical energy created when it fought, fled, or froze immediately after reaching safety by shaking or another physiological movement. This "discharges" the trauma and the terrorizing event is not stored in the body (Levine, 1997).

Human beings, however, often do not release that energy after surviving a traumatic event. This stored trauma makes them more vulnerable to re-acting to a nonthreatening situation as if the past danger was present. Even though no current threat exists, the reactions produced by the lower-level brain—fight, flight, or freeze—overpower higher-level brain functions like reasoning and decision making. To release oneself from this cycle, Levine recommends "pendulation," a tool to unlock and release stored trauma (Levine, 1997). Pendulation involves a client shifting mental focus from positive to negative experiences, ultimately returning to positive ones. This mental movement frees the trapped somatic energy, releasing the involuntary reactions (of the body) associated with the traumatic event.

Parker, Doctor, and Selvam (2008) found that Somatic Experiencing Therapy was effective in treating trauma in tsunami survivors. Therapists helped participants increase their awareness of traumatic body reactions while also building feelings of connections and safety with the therapist. Participants described memories—what they felt and did—and their body's reactions to these memories. This process helped to release the involuntary body reactions associated with the traumatic event.

Cognitive Behavior Therapy (CBT)

Judith Beck developed cognitive behavior therapy (CBT) in the early 1960s and throughout his career demonstrated the close relationship between our thoughts, feelings, and behavior (2011). Beck enlisted clients as active participants in the process of understanding and changing their beliefs and behavior. For example, clients are asked to observe what automatically comes to mind in reaction to an idea or event, such as thinking about hanging out with friends and then having the automatic thought that the friends don't want to hang out. The therapist asks the client to explore feelings (such as depression and anxiety) that follow that thought ("my friends don't want me around"): The insight sheds light on the client's current behavior of avoiding friends. This kind of analysis is continued during therapy sessions and in homework assigned by the therapist.

Clients participate in selecting problems to work on during therapy (Beck, 2011). Their core beliefs (like being competent versus dumb) were developed from earlier experiences and relationships. These beliefs color how one interprets life events. When core beliefs are negative, a client experiences current situations with sadness, discouragement, and hopelessness. Selecting a problem to work on may help a client to feel more hopeful, especially when the solution is broken down into manageable steps to avoid feeling, overwhelmed (Beck, 2011). Being an active participant also challenges any core beliefs that one is a failure or that personal efforts are futile.

In CBT, the therapist's goals are to identify automatic thoughts and assumptions, then explain how they lead to certain feelings and repeated behaviors. When the client develops an awareness of the links between thinking, feeling, and acting, then behaviors can be changed. With this awareness, core beliefs can be altered so that clients will lead happier and more peaceful lives.

Dialectic Behavior Therapy (DBT)

In Dialectic Behavior Therapy (DBT), disorders of emotional dysregulation are viewed as resulting from transactions between a person's emotional vulnerability and another's invalidating social responses toward her (Linehan, 1993). This intervention combines behavior change strategies with acceptance principles. During DBT, a client's skills are enhanced (mindfulness, emotional regulation, toleration of distress, and interpersonal skills) and the therapist encourages motivation to generalize these skills in everyday life and to improve past problematic behavior. The family and social environment are a focus with a goal that they facilitate treatment rather than impede it.

Since invalidation is an important component of the criticism and disrespect in domestic abuse, Iverson, Shenk, and Fruzzetti (2009) have applied DBT to interventions with battered women. They view the communication couples experience during domestic violence as including nonacceptance and verbal abuse of the victim, which creates an unsafe and stressful environment. This can increase a victim's negative emotions like depression, anxiety, and hopelessness, both in the abusive relationship itself and in larger contexts, a generalizability that can persist even after the relationship is over. During these groups for battered women, DBT was used to develop new skills, further utilize old skills, analyze and practice problem solving, apply skills to everyday life, and plan opportunities to use more effective and skillful behaviors. Women enjoyed validation and encouragement from group members and the therapist. The authors describe improved emotional regulation and functioning among the participants.

Theater

Vygotsky supported the importance of social learning and imitation in the development of children (1934). His principles have been applied to psychotherapy by Lois Holzman, who emphasizes the unity of cognitive and emotional learning in therapy (2013).

Social therapy is based on individual development in the context of group creativity. There is a blending and unity of learning and development, intellectual and affective growth. Clients learn while being supported by the therapist and other group members in a group therapy setting. The model is that children learn in a collective environment with others. Group therapy involves the support of members toward each other, as well as learning from others in the context of developing the group.

Murray Dabby (M. Dabby, personal interview, November 13, 2014) is a social therapist who studied with Holzman. During therapy, Dabby evaluates and treats people by observing more than what is said, as clients share their experiences. In a group setting, he also watches their use of the body, intention, passion, desire, and cognitive thinking. Performance exercises are applied in these groups so that members can support each other during the process of changing feelings and thoughts, which leads to improvement in anxiety, trauma, and other problems.

For example, in his improv-therapy groups for social anxiety, Dabby asked a shy group member to imagine her favorite hero. Then she was instructed to be that hero while attending a cocktail party improvised by other group members who also played their hero characters. This client, fearful of social interaction, chose a dancer as her hero, prancing around at the make-believe cocktail party with a sense of fun and enjoyment. She did not discuss any previous trauma. Instead, she performed without anxiety, and subsequent reports by this client indicated that she changed how she viewed herself after this repeated experience and her humor and whimsy manifested in a way that she never imagined possible.

Other group members were asked by the leader to be very supportive and encouraging. The dancing client received feedback that was encouraging and complimentary—more than she imagined was possible. The others may have told her that she was creative and daring, which she would remember long afterward.

Dabby described new memories as being imprinted so that the dancing client would remember all of the positive reinforcement. And memories are additive, so they build confidence and self-assurance. One humorless client began cracking jokes during the improv (unscripted event) and was, for the first time, considered delightful and funny.

During some skits, Dabby acts as the director and creates different experiences for the expression of feelings. For one very stiff person with a trauma history, he asked her to tell about her life while playing a tipsy person with others in a bar during an earthquake. She did so with great humor, hanging on the furniture and wobbling during the earthquake. People tend to be very affected by these experiences, according to Dabby, so that they deal with problems in ways that do not re-traumatize them.

Van der Kolk (2014) discussed using the theater to help change patterns of thinking. One example is Urban Improvisation where there are scripted skits that contain descriptions of common problems such as jealousy. While acting out these scripts, the action can stop at the point where a choice is involved. For example, someone feeling jealous could choose behavior A or behavior B. A discussion can be used to explore various options, and volunteers may be involved in demonstrating alternative behavioral choices as well.

THE CHALLENGE OF EMOTIONAL REGULATION
IN THE MIDST OF TRAUMA AND COERCION

When children, adolescents, and adults experience traumatic events, they are often flooded with feelings and overwhelmed with anxiety and terror. Reacting as if the past traumatic events are occurring over and over in the present, the traumatized live in an automatic terror mode. Inner arousal continues to embrace and drive them, often leaving little energy or focus for such activities as school studies, job performance, or social interaction. Instead, feelings spill over and the terror leaves them paralyzed, fighting back, and/or fleeing from horrors within. For the coerced, horrors come from without as well; the coerced are weighted down in mind, body, and spirit with continuous threats and possibilities of danger.

Traumatized people often search for peace and relief from past memories, sensations, and perceived danger. For the traumatized coerced, the perceived danger may well involve past trauma, but the perception and terror certainly involve the present, as well. Whether forced into illegal activity or shoved into other behaviors unaligned with one's own values and heartfelt beliefs, many of the coerced grasp at a sense of self and connection with others while slipping away from the familiar. Lost from even themselves, they are emotional wanderers in the night, hoping for an awakening from their nightmare but stuck in the shadow of inner guilt and horror. Cognitive confusion abounds: The coerced are often expected to make reasonable decisions in the midst of unreasonable demands and racing thoughts, clouded by the certainty of danger for themselves, loved ones, and innocent others. Safety for traumatized, coerced individuals comes from understanding coercive dynamics, escape to freedom (even if that means arrest), and interventions that recognize and treat trauma and coercion.

Various types of trauma treatment have been explored in this chapter as if each is a separate process and endeavor. In practice however, a therapist may use multiple therapeutic interventions. As suggested by Rasche, some of these interventions can be combined to help with the overactivity of a traumatized individual's brain and the need for relaxation and processing of the memories and sensations that are stuck in the mind (C. Rasche, personal interview, November 13, 2014). Research from the Trauma Center at the Justice Resource Institute (JRI) in Boston reflects contemporary creative exploration into various areas for treating trauma, including yoga, neurofeedback, EMDR, and theater.

Research includes efficacy studies, such as which types of intervention were more effective in helping traumatized youth and adults. In a preliminary study on the use of sensory motor arousal regulation treatment (SMART), sensory regulation was used with youth as an avenue to help with behavioral and emotional regulation (Warner et al., 2014). Youth in a residential treatment facility used a specially designed room with floor mats and specific exercise equipment. Therapists worked with the traumatized youth to recognize behaviors contributing to their overarousal and they searched together for calming physical activities. One youth talked a great deal about his past abuse and his own abusive behaviors toward a family member—talking so much about it that the therapist noticed these discussions only added to his anxiety and overarousal. They explored together which physical activities helped calm the youth, so that he could regulate his own emotions. The therapist and youth succeeded in decreasing his overwhelming anxiety and other trauma symptoms, leading to greater knowledge and mastery by the youth.

Therapeutic Intervention with the Coerced

Therapeutic intervention with the coerced will be discussed later. Trauma interventions described in this chapter can be used if the coerced are overcome with trauma. By understanding coercion and restoring the fractured self, many of the coerced experience a greater sense of hope and peace. Their confusion and self-blame is replaced by growing clarity and integration of the self. Hungry and yearning for connection, warmth, acceptance, and encouragement, the coerced can discover an escape from captivity—whether that escape involves arrest, separation from the coercer, or finding more freedom and safety within the relationship.

3

Recognizing
Intimate Coercion

In her poem "Flee on Your Donkey," Anne Sexton (1966) describes her dreams as fighters coming into the ring while she looks at emptiness stretching miles downward. She tries to pull her dreams up from the emptiness while feeling deep hunger and longing. Coercion is like that, stealing dreams and leaving a deep abyss of confusion, hunger, and longing. Many of the coerced are unable to describe their horror, caught in unspeakable anguish and despair. As described by van der Kolk, their bodies keep the score of their trauma, marking their lives with physical illness that carries pain and discomfort of the trauma (van der Kolk, 2014).

THREATS AND HARM

Intimate coercion involves threats and actual harm designed to force a person into certain behaviors. Why would someone want to force his partner into any behavior? Just the idea of forcing must mean that the person does not *want* to behave that way. And what kind of relationship has one person unable to voice her own ideas and carry out her own choices? Being forced seems like the opposite of a loving relationship in which one is supported during activities and relationships. The coerced's sadness and sorrow stem from the heartlessness of being threatened and forced into unwanted behaviors. And despair grows from not being allowed to follow dreams and develop personal values and ideas so that they blossom and show her real self to the world.

Betsy's Loss of Her Dream

Loring conducted an evaluation of Betsy after her lawyer called asking for help. Betsy had studied drama in college and dreamed of becoming an actress. She worked for several years as a waitress, getting more and more acting roles, both in her own city and out-of-town. When she started dating Bill, he seemed to support her acting, reading through scripts with her after he'd get home from work. Later they married and, when she started getting more out-of-town roles, he began to complain, shouting that she was selfish and inconsiderate; and he insisted that she was not willing to compromise and be part of a family. Betsy believed him, seeing herself as a poor wife—an accusation she often heard from Bill.

Betsy had not been aware that Bill used drugs before they married. However, he began to bring cocaine to their house, insisting that Betsy join him in using the drug. When she refused to participate, Bill threatened to leave her. He cut Betsy off from her family, saying she was too dependent on her parents. Bill often slapped her and called Betsy names like "stupid" and "worthless." He limited her telephone calls by taking away her cell phone so that their landline was the only way she could talk with her parents. Bill would listen to her telephone conversations. She felt isolated and missed working in a restaurant since Bill wanted her at home all the time. She also missed acting.

Bill threatened to harm her miniature poodle. On one occasion when Betsy got a small part acting in a nearby theater, Bill told her she would never see her dog again. The small dog disappeared and Bill refused to give Betsy any information, although he admitted causing the disappearance. Betsy yielded to his pressure and became involved with cocaine. The dog was returned by Bill. He gave her occasional praise, but Betsy felt depressed since using drugs was actually against her own values. When police followed Bill home from buying drugs, they raided and searched their home, finding cocaine in a bag taped underneath a table. Both were arrested. During her psychosocial evaluation, Betsy expressed her feeling of being lost.

> Parts of myself were eroding away, like you see soil washed away on a river bank. I lost confidence in myself and was afraid for Bill to leave me. I believed it when he said I couldn't survive without him. I felt like I was in the same cage as my dream of acting. I knew he'd make my dog disappear like he said. So I just followed orders.

TYPES OF ABUSE THAT ACCOMPANY COERCION

Physical Abuse

Many of the coerced describe being hit, slapped, shoved, pushed, punched, choked, thrown against the wall, and hit with objects. Physical abuse can encompass a range of behaviors: Tying up or hanging someone by some part of their body, slamming a body against something, burning, freezing, cutting, scraping, spitting, twisting, and any other assault to the body. It can also include shoving food or forcing liquid into someone's mouth or into the eyes or nose or pulling someone by the hair. In these cases, more than the body is hurt. This type of physical abuse hurts the person's feelings and sense of worth, as well as damaging her sense of trust.

Loring found during her evaluations with the coerced that they often feel a deep sense of disappointment. In relationships, they seek love and trust, happiness and hope, shared planning and experiences. But this is not what they have found. Rather, the physical abuse leaves a sense of doubt and fear: Coerced individuals wonder, "What will I be forced to do next?"

For many of the coerced, any harm or threat of harm to their pets or children is even more horrible than their own wounds. Hitting, punching, throwing, kicking, withholding food from children and dogs (or other animals) is not unusual when coercion is present. Research has shown that harm to children and pets was associated with women's obedience to the orders of a coercer (Loring and Beaudoin, 2000). In that study, many women said they were less afraid of being harmed themselves and more terrified of physical abuse to their beloved children and pets.

Beverly Protects Her Son

Beverly's husband, Rob, was a drug addict. Rob believed that his father, a wealthy banker, had always been critical of him, so Rob decided to rob his father's bank. Rob ordered Beverly to drive him to the bank that he had decided to rob. She knew nothing about his plans.

The night before the robbery, Rob slapped and threw their six-year-old son, Matthew, across the room. When Beverly rushed to her son's aid, Rob pointed a gun at her and told Beverly and Matthew that, from now on, he was going to get respect in his home—and that meant obedience. He ordered Matthew to go to bed, even though it was six o'clock and no one had eaten dinner. And he informed Beverly that she would drive him to cash a check at the bank the next day. While Beverly wondered what check he had received, she had learned from past experience not to question his orders, or he would punch her in the stomach where black and blue bruises would not show.

The next day, after Matthew went to school, Beverly drove Rob to the bank. He told her to wait in the car, that he'd be right back. She was surprised when he stepped out of the car and she spotted the bulge in his jacket pocket. She had seen that same bulge the night before when Rob pulled the gun from his jacket and aimed it at her. Before closing the car door, Rob ordered her to wait for him and not speak to anyone. Rob added that she would follow his orders and wait there for him, or he'd kill their son.

Beverly did not remember waiting in the car, or even Rob hopping back in and ordering her to drive away. She recalled parts of the drive home and the police arriving that night to arrest both of them for the bank robbery. Beverly later explained that she was so anxious that time seemed to fly by and she did not remember much while she waited for Rob at the bank.

> I was so scared he'd kill Matthew. I did everything he said. But I never thought he'd rob the bank. What if he'd hurt a teller? I sat there in the car. It seemed like time was racing by. I don't even remember him getting back in the car.

Often coupled with threats of harm or death, physical abuse is a powerful tool used by coercers to force obedience to their orders. The terror of those being coerced can rise to the level of shock and horror, often interfering with memory and thinking. How would a woman stop to think about alternatives when her son's life depended on certain behavior—following specific orders? During the evaluation, Beverly said she couldn't think of any alternatives because she believed that Rob would kill their son if she disobeyed.

Sexual Abuse

Some abusers coerce women into unwanted sexual behaviors. When forced to perform sexual acts or go to unwanted sites of various sexual activities, many coerced women experience feelings of fear and dread, degradation and humiliation.

Andi's Embarrassment and Fear

Andi is a fifty-four-year-old college professor, well known for her research and teaching. At her college, reputation is important. The conservative philosophy of the school made it an attractive choice for many parents and students. So it was risky when Andi's husband, Jason, began visiting strip bars in a neighboring city, as well as insisting that Andi accompany him. He threatened to write an anonymous note to the college president, accusing Andi of being a prostitute unless she accompanied him to strip bars where:

> there were sexual activities she did not want to see;
> she saw illegal drug and sexual behaviors she feared could damage her reputation;
> she felt sick to her stomach when she saw young women, some of whom appeared to be drunk and exploited;
> she was scared there would be students who would discover her there;

she was embarrassed when her husband paid women to do lap dances
   and allow him to touch them intimately; and
she constantly looked around for people who could impact her job.

What other kind of threats could have convinced Andi to go along
with her husband, Jason, and his sexual escapades? During Loring's
evaluation, Andi revealed that Jason was physically abusive, punching
and slapping Andi when he went into rages. He never hit her in the face
where bruises would show. Relatives, friends, and colleagues confirmed
that Andi was isolated, rarely attending family or faculty events. And on
rare occasions when she went to a party, Jason could be seen clutching
her arm at all times and monitoring her conversations. A new car dealer,
Jason bought a dealership and hired plenty of helpers, giving him time to
watch over Andi and their two young daughters.

During the psychosocial evaluation, Andi described Jason's continuous
criticisms of her as a "bad mother," "neglectful wife," and "uptight Puri-
tan." He accused her of withholding normal sexual exploration and ruin-
ing his life and their marriage. Later, the daughters confirmed separately
that their dad hit Andi and called her a poor mother and wife.

The sex bar was raided because a great deal of drug activity was going
on there. Jason had slipped an envelope into Andi's purse at the beginning of the evening: "Money in case we get low on funds," he had told
her. During the police search, the envelope in her purse was discovered. It
contained drugs and they both were charged with drug possession. During an interview with Loring, Jason admitted that he had put the drugs in
her purse. He also recalled that he had often threatened to divorce Andi
and take away their children, saying that she'd never see her daughters
again. Please note that it is not always possible to talk when someone
is represented by another lawyer, but in this case, Jason insisted that he
meet Andi's evaluator.

Many in Andi's community asked: Why would a woman allow herself
to be manipulated by such a man? Why would Andi even have gone to
the bar? Coerced behavior, however, can never be seen alone. Rather, it
must be viewed in the context of abuse and coercion. Only then will the
full extent of fear behind that single act be discovered. To rob a bank out
of greed for money is one type of behavior. To drive your husband to a
bank for fear he'll harm or kill your child if you refuse—that is a very
different thing.

Emotional Abuse

"Emotional abuse is an ongoing process in which one individual systematically diminishes and destroys the inner self of another. The essential
ideas, feelings, perceptions, and personality characteristics of the victim

are constantly belittled. Eventually the victim begins to experience these aspects of the self as seriously eroded or absent" (Loring, 1994). Emotional abuse during coercion involves a betrayal of trust when an intimate partner shoves the coerced into dangerous situations and illegal behavior with terrible consequences. Or the coerced may be shoved into legal behaviors that are not in keeping with her comfort, values, or dreams. According to Evan Stark, "Coercion entails the use of force or threats to compel or dispel a particular response" (Stark, 2007, p. 228). Stark explains that coercion is not always shouted from the roof tops, but can include subtle threats and "other forms of intimidation where the threat of force is implied rather than explicit" (Stark, 2007, p. 228).

During Loring's evaluations, it often became clear that a threat could be whispered, written, or shared with a symbolic gesture, like a finger drawn from one side of the neck to the other side, suggesting that violence might be just around the corner. Physical abuse often accompanies coercion, but coercion can exist without any physical abuse at all. When a woman believes that her partner can carry out his threats, especially when those threats rock her to the core, she is forced into obedience. Everyone has certain treasures in life. For some women, the treasures include a loving relationship with her beloved parents; for others, it may be their children and pets; or a job; or some precious qualities they have worked hard to develop in themselves, like excellence in teaching or parenting. Hopes and dreams for the future are embraced by many. As accurate as a radar detecting device, a coercer focuses on one or more of those treasures and dreams. Sometimes the woman has confided her treasures to him. Other times her love and adoration of her children, pet, other animals, friends, and relatives is evident for all to observe.

Elaine Wants to Protect Her Mother

Loring's evaluation of Elaine occurred after she had delivered a package for her husband. She had been observed by an undercover police officer who seized the package and found drugs hidden inside. When Elaine's home was searched by police, it was discovered that her husband, Ted, had been selling drugs, delivering cocaine to people in packages labeled with the names of the buyers. Obeying Ted's command to perform this act, Elaine was charged with serious drug crimes.

> I dreamed of a close relationship with my mom. I hoped we'd write poetry together. Maybe even publish it. I was scared Ted would kill my mom. He said he'd take her out in the country. Maybe would push her out of the car while he was driving fast. My mom has dementia. Even if he left her alone in the country, that'd be awful. So I delivered his package. I never thought about what was in it.

4

The Foundation of
Intimate Coercion

Evan Stark (2007) has described opposition to subjugation of any kind as based on the same reasoning that leads us to oppose coercion, since people should be treated as ends in themselves, whose dignity, freedom, and worth merit the fullest support. Just as the foundation supports a house, several processes interweave like a tapestry to create intimate coercion. These underlying processes work together, preventing intervention by those trying to lead the woman away from harm.

BELIEF IN HARM

A woman drowning in coercion feels like she is suffocating, unable to escape the threatened harm to herself and to her loved ones. Much like someone flailing about in a deep body of water, her focus is on staying above the surface. She is certain that great harm is a reality that could occur at any moment: The coerced feel a sense of urgency about impending harm; there is no doubt about whether or not it will happen. The main question is when and how will harm occur and whether there is any way of delaying it.

Susan's Hopes for Delay

Susan, a sixty-two-year-old retired accountant, remarried soon after her previous husband died. Her new husband, Jed, was a retired banker who had many ideas about how to invest Susan's considerable wealth. Any

27

hesitance on Susan's part would result in his becoming angry and accusing her of having no confidence in him. While he never physically hit her, Jed would ignore and shun her, going away from the home for days at a time. Susan feared abandonment. She had grown up in foster care after her father abandoned the family and her mother became heavily involved with drugs, often spending food money for various drugs.

After years in foster care, sixteen-year-old Susan was adopted, yet she never escaped the fear of loss in relationships. Jed had discovered this and exploited it to force Susan's compliance with his orders. His threats to leave Susan resulted in her allowing him to change her investments, bit by bit, until he was withdrawing large amounts of money, keeping a sizeable portion to spend and investing the rest in ways that allowed him quick access to the money.

Jed said he would leave Susan if she did not comply with his financial planning. He took a few test runs by disappearing for days at a time, with no calls to check in with Susan. Her two adult daughters lived in separate homes with their own families. They watched helplessly, aware of what was happening but unable to change it. Susan had previously arranged for her two daughters to receive monthly statements about the investments so they witnessed the diminishing estate.

Yet any questions from them were met by Susan's explanations that Jed was a great investor and they would see the estate making money soon. Not that she had a great deal of time to consult with them because Jed called her away from conversations with her daughters after a brief amount of time passed. He listened when Susan spoke to them on the telephone and was present whenever they visited the home.

For Susan, threats of being abandoned were terrifying. Her daughters could imagine nothing more constructive than for Jed to leave, to get out of their lives. This belief in a great harm is characteristic of the coerced. The scope of that harm is defined by the coerced in relation to their past pain and current hopes and treasures. Coercers explore the vulnerabilities of a woman to discover what the most painful threats would be, uncovering the present treasures—love for a child, pet, family member, career, house, artwork. The coercer's threats to harm are believed by the frightened coerced, like Susan.

> I don't know when it started, but I got to the point where I felt like I had no choice. Jed said he knew the best way to invest. My investment broker and sister and daughters didn't trust him. He said I had to trust him or I was a poor excuse of a wife. It got to where I rarely talked with family alone. Jed was always there. If they brought up finances, we'd leave because he insisted. I was scared all the time. I just tried to get him to wait to reinvest the large portions of my money.

Family members often feel helpless when they observe a loved one being coerced. Although they may try to influence the situation, the coercer has captured their loved one, isolating and dominating even a formerly strong and independent woman.

DISSOLUTION OF THE SELF

Believing the accusations and labels, many coerced women see themselves as "stupid" or "worthless," lacking in some way, not as knowledgeable as the coercer. That is what she has been told, and then, internalizing the labels and accusations, she believes it. Acceptance of the negativity and degradation leads to the fracturing of her self. Just as one would break an arm, the structure and sense of self has been broken.

Marie-France Hirigoyen (2000) has described emotional abuse in a parent toward a child: "The parent doesn't actually kill his child, but annihilates him by diminishing his identity until the child becomes nothing" (p. 47). Similarly, B. Lempert (1989) depicted the feeling of no longer being—the annihilation of the soul. Susan, described above, experienced this fractured self, a sense of being annihilated. "I just felt like nothing. No inner voice spoke up. He kept taking my money. I tried to delay him. I felt dead inside. And scared he'd leave me."

The coerced, like Susan, often had past experiences that mirror the current coercion. Of course, coercion can occur to a woman who has not been involved with it before. But many of the coerced are revisiting a helpless, frightening position in their lives.

Mandy's Experience of Degradation

As an attorney, Mandy represented people in trouble with the law. They had committed different crimes: Theft, stock fraud, embezzlement, assault, even murder. She was seen as being very effective in the courtroom, conveying information in an energetic and convincing manner. When her new husband began physically abusing her, few knew about it. Before their marriage, he had slapped her twice and apologized each time. She believed his promises that he would get counseling and that it would not happen again.

His threats to Mandy included divorce and filing for custody of their nine-year-old son, Brandon. He called her a "lousy mother" who was a danger to Brandon because she failed to protect him. Terrified of losing her son—and believing his many accusations of poor mothering—Mandy felt depressed and lost. He demanded that she call each hour when she went out with friends and monitored her telephone conversations. Mandy discussed her feelings with two friends at work, lawyers who were furious about his false accusations. Yet, Mandy was so shaken by continuous emotional abuse that she was unable to embrace her friends' reassurances.

She felt confused and wondered if he was right about her poor mothering. His criticisms continued: He did not like how she dressed, spoke, kept house, and related to people—Mandy experienced a sense of having lost her self. "I lost my confidence. Even in court, I second guessed myself. I listened to my husband about what was best for my son."

ISOLATION

When the coercer has betrayed the trust of the coerced, has threatened abandonment, harm, even death, the caring connection between them is broken. Jean Baker Miller (1988) at the Stone Center described this disrupted connection.

> I believe that the most terrifying and destructive feeling that a person can experience is isolation. This is not the same as "being alone" in the more straightforward sense. It is feeling locked out of the possibility of human connection. This feeling of desperate loneliness is usually accompanied by the feeling that you, yourself, are the reason for the exclusion. It is because of who you are. And you feel helpless, powerless, unable to act to change the situation. People will do almost anything to escape this combination of condemned isolation and powerless.

Louise Considered Suicide

Louise, a hotel manager, felt desperate, powerless, and suicidal during her marriage to Al.

> Things went well at first. Neither of us had children and we spent a lot of time hiking together. Then Al became really critical of me. He didn't like the way I did the wash, cleaned the house, bought groceries. I didn't even get some of his criticism right from him. My friends would tell me that he'd said bad things about me, real sarcastic-like. I felt desperate to get back the sense of closeness I thought we'd had. But there were always strings attached. To be close, Al said I had to pay more attention to him and less to my sisters and parents. I had to bring him home samples of shampoo and stuff from hotel rooms. It didn't feel honest to me, but I did it. I got really scared when he told me to bring a painting out of a room. He wanted it in his car to sell. I did it. I took the painting to avoid his ignoring me for days. Before, when I didn't do what he said, he wouldn't talk to me. Or hug me. I'd feel like killing myself.

SURVEILLANCE

Surveillance is part of the foundation holding up coercion. It can be clear and obvious, like actually following and monitoring the coerced, who observes this stalking behavior. Or the surveillance may not be observed. The coercer later tells his partner about her own behavior, often in great detail. The coerced woman knows that the only way her actions could be known is through surveillance. Afterward, she feels a continuous sense of being watched and often looks over her shoulder, wondering what consequences she will face for various behaviors.

Evan Stark (2007) describes the contours of micro-surveillance. Controlling partners view intimate relations as a zero-sum game in which any sign of a partner's separateness is interpreted as something taken from them. Looking to detect disobedience or disloyalty, they may survey the minute facets of a woman's everyday conduct until choice itself becomes frightening. This surveillance can include counting the number of miles driven, attaching a listening device to the telephone, having the coerced call home every so many minutes when out of the home, forcing the coerced to always answer the telephone when called by the coercer, no matter how dangerous or inconvenient.

These and other forms of surveillance can also pose a danger to the woman's innocent coworkers, family members, friends, and neighbors. If the coercer feels betrayed and abandoned, himself, he may become enraged and if he has access to weapons, there is danger to all.

RITUALIZED EMOTIONAL ABUSE

Ritualized emotional abuse is often a vital element in the foundation of coercion. Once a series of actions becomes established, the coerced experiences terror at step one or two rather than waiting until step five or six. The end result is apparent almost immediately to someone who has experienced the series of events in that ritual, step by step. A coercer first threatens to harm a child, then goes to the closet to select a weapon, grabs a knife, walks into the child's room, calls for the woman to come watch, warns her not to call police or he will have killed the child by the time they arrive, and threatens by placing a knife to the child's throat with one hand and drawing the fingers on the other hand across his own neck. Afterward, all that has to happen is for him to draw fingers across his neck and a woman may feel coerced into obeying his orders.

This makes the coercion even more hidden from others. Who among us is likely to become agitated over someone simply rubbing the front of his neck? Or someone whispering something in a partner's ear or tapping their shoulder? When these first steps signal the following behaviors in a ritualized string of actions, then the coerced may panic. The quick neck rub (when that has led to her or her child being choked), tapping of the shoulder (if that has previously preceded his taking the child away for days at a time), or whispering (threats to kill the child) constitute a hidden language that is not always evident to others.

Cindy's Constant Anxiety

When Cindy worked as director of a child care center, the parents agreed they could count on their children being safe, learning new things, and enjoying themselves. The center grew and grants supported some of the creative programs. But after her marriage to Mike, Cindy found it hard to concentrate, always looking over her shoulder to see if Mike was watching. When he visited the center, she watched him carefully to observe any of the motions that would signal violence to her or their son later in the evening.

Her coworkers noticed some of his put downs and disrespect toward Cindy, but they were not aware of the dangerous threats. Mike said he would kill Cindy and their young son, Peter, and bury both of them in a national forest. Cindy believed his threats because Mike had described murdering a man named Stanton and showed her newspaper articles about Stanton's murder.

> I might have been wrong. I believed Mike would kill us. He'd wipe the sweat off his forehead. I'd panic. That was the first thing he'd do. Then he'd get his gun and point it at me and my son.

Mike gained access to the child care center by compelling Cindy to give him the key. He stole money and equipment. After an investigation, they were both arrested; Cindy said she felt relieved and grateful to have been arrested and saved.

DISTAL COERCION

During a particular evaluation, a woman expressed that she was frightened to discuss drug trafficking by her boyfriend, the reason for her arrest. She was willing to talk about the way he threatened and beat her but not the types of drugs and how he distributed them. Her husband, a drug kingpin, was staying in a different country for a while. Indeed, she had accompanied him on some of his drug delivery trips, but was afraid to discuss it.

This situation was an example of distal coercion—he was threatening her from afar—but authorities doubted that someone so far away could inspire fear. Yet, the distance does not matter when the often-repeated threats by the coercer replay continually in the woman's head; or threats continue during telephone conversations and/or in his messages (from others, via the Internet, or in letters). In this case, one such threat involved him hiring someone nearby to kidnap and kill her. Another drug smuggler's girlfriend had suffered that same fate in the past. Fortunately, law enforcement eventually believed her concerns.

DELAYING METHODS

The coerced cannot always escape threats, but delaying or lessening them may be possible. A coping method used by some of the coerced is to delay or only seem to be obeying an order whenever the threats become unbearable.

Allie delayed sneaking valuable paintings out of the museum where she worked. She would tell her boyfriend that she had tried, but security guards had followed her. When he threatened her child with harm, she would buy some art objects from the museum gift store and pretend to have stolen them.

Not all coercive behaviors aim at compelling a woman to participate in illegal behaviors. Some coercion has as its aim forcing the woman into sexual, emotional, or physical behaviors that she opposes; these behaviors may be alien to her value system. Andi, described previously, was coerced into going with her husband to strip bars. Her husband's threat involved kidnapping their child. Some of the coerced have described delaying these unwanted activities by feigning illness or using work meetings to delay participation.

TUNNEL VISION AND DISSOCIATION

Coerced women can obey orders without seeing the wider context or ultimate purpose of their behaviors. Trauma and terror often cause the coerced to focus narrowly on the demands, without being able to give much thought to the final objectives. To ask about objectives can result in the coercer's rage, because he frequently interprets such questions as doubting him, a lack of loyalty, even refusal to obey.

This tunnel vision is usually caused by absorption, an undue focus of attention on a very narrow part of an experience. Absorption and other forms of dissociation occur among children and adults. Some children dissociate in order to survive abuse that is more than they can bear. One client described his childhood sexual abuse, forced to behave sexually with his sisters by a brutal stepfather; he felt that he was not present during the forced behavior, and would stare into space to shut out the horrors, occasionally seeing a circus with animals and people performing on the ceiling.

Steele, Boon, and van der Hart described three types of dissociation: (1) People may space out with a narrow field of attention, what can be called tunnel vision or absorption, in which certain aspects of an experience are addressed while others are not. For example, the coerced may obey orders without being aware of their consequences, only focused on the behavior of "doing"; (2) They may shut down emotionally and physically, which is an automatic physiological reaction much like the possum playing dead. Such a person is extremely numb, only going through the motions, unaware of feelings or thoughts. In fact, in this state, one is unable to think so the coerced person may act like an automaton; (3) people may have a sense of self that is more or less divided or fragmented, which is the original and most accurate definition of dissociation. Whatever experience may be encoded in a person's normal sense of self (for example, the adult, functional self that knows something is wrong) may not be remembered when the person is in a different sense of self (the coerced self that is subjugated and has tunnel vision or is shut down) (Kathy Steele, personal interview, February 9, 2015). Many of the coerced who experience this amnesia cannot accurately remember all aspects of the coerced activity. The coerced may not remember what they have said, heard, seen, done, felt, or thought—logically assuming they saw or did something but having no actual memory of it. Or they may have a vague awareness, as though it happened to someone else.

Dissociative people are often also highly hypnotizable. This means they are very vulnerable to coercive suggestions and orders, and some can even hallucinate something away. That is, they literally do not see what actually is there (Kathy Steele, personal interview, February 9, 2015).

Sally's Tunnel Vision

Sally was much younger than her husband who demanded her continuous attention to his legal briefs, housework, cooking, and sexual activity. She was never to question, only to obey. He isolated her more and more from family and friends. When they were arrested and accused of making a bomb that harmed a businessman, Sally was not able to believe that she had copied threatening notes (without looking at them as he had ordered) or purchased some bomb parts—been part of a plot to harm someone.

At first, Sally denied that her husband could have committed such violence. During the evaluation, she began to recognize the certainty that he had sent threatening letters and a bomb that harmed a businessman whom he resented, feeling cheated by this person. Sally felt anguish and despair, horrified that she had assisted with the plot. She would stare into space for periods of time, later explaining that she felt more anxiety than she could handle. Sally was dissociating to get away from these intolerable feelings. She described herself as usually seeing the whole picture of any event and skillful at multitasking, able to accomplish several tasks at once. Yet, while being threatened by her husband, Sally had only seen the task she was working on at a given moment and was unaware of bomb making in the home. After a great deal of time spent working with Sally and listening to her descriptions of ordered activities, law enforcement officers began to believe that coercion had occurred. They noticed that she at first denied that her husband could have committed the violence, but later acknowledged her role in assisting him—much to her own horror.

HIDDEN AND DENIED ABUSE

Out in the open, abuse has a clarity that is understood by the coerced. It may be dangerous and devastating, but not confusing. Threats and name-calling are clear and vivid. Sometimes the woman is blamed for the violence, told that her own behavior has caused the coercer to behave in a given way. This is puzzling to the coerced person, who has done nothing to deserve the verbal and/or physical abuse. She may be told later that this abusive coercion never occurred, which adds to her confusion.

When cruelty is disguised, denied, and blamed on the coerced woman, she becomes desperate to understand and believe in her own thinking; she is mixed up and sometimes even feels like she is losing her mind, an accusation often used by coercers. When he casts doubt on her thinking, problem solving, and perceptions, the coercer then takes over as the one who determines reality and assigns blame and failure. An integral part of emotional abuse, this process involves denial and disregard of another's needs: For the coerced, there is a sense of being invisible or "disappeared."

Janice Walks on Quicksand

Janice and her husband, Paul, are psychologists. Paul charged insurance companies for tests he never performed. The administrator of their practice billed for Paul's supposed tests and the other professionals in their practice group wondered how he could perform so many tests when Paul did not work full-time. Seen by others as a skilled therapist, Janice felt confused and saddened by Paul's behavior.

> Paul criticized me all the time and, when I'd confront him, he'd say that he never was critical, that I was such a poor wife, cook, companion that he couldn't overlook it. That's what he said. I felt like I was walking on quicksand. Anything I'd say was fuel for his degrading remarks. He even said I was a lousy sex partner, but had no ideas about what he wanted different. I felt a sense of futility, of despair.

Sadness is common among the coerced, as well as a sense of despair and hopelessness. It is important to question the coerced about whether self-harm has been considered, because many feel trapped and see no way to escape. Their anguish is painful with no end in sight. Questions should include whether they think about harming themselves or others (like children), whether they have a plan to accomplish this, and if they believe they would actually follow the plan. Many answer "no," that they would not do so. There is usually a reason for not completing a plan, for example, that they would never hurt their children or betray God in this fashion.

Coercion is betrayal of loving connection and degradation of the coerced. With a language and symbolism of its own, coercion has a foundation in the coerced's belief in harm, dissolution of the self, broken connections, surveillance, ritualized emotional abuse, distal coercion, tunnel vision, delaying methods, and hidden and denied abuse. Imagine the relief and clarity when, as will be described, a coerced person becomes aware of this foundation and all of its components. Some have described this awareness as a sense of clarity, emotional freedom, and hopefulness.

5

A Closer Look
at the Coerced

In his poetry, Coleridge (1950) wrote about profound grief experienced as a dark and dreary void with no outlet or relief (p. 170). The coerced are caught in a dark void where grief is not always visible to others. A coerced woman may appear calm and clear-thinking; she may appear to perform well in her job; others may see her as caring toward friends and family. However, most coerced women are frightened, looking over their shoulder for the controller's dominating rule, and saddened at the loss of their life's dream.

TRAUMA AMONG THE COERCED

Most coerced women suffer from trauma, leading to overwhelming anxiety that floods the mind and body. Memories of traumatic events can also cause withdrawal from any reminder of the event. As discussed previously, a traumatized woman may dissociate—lose awareness of the environment—usually when anxiety is too severe and coping becomes difficult (American Psychiatric Association, 2013). Conversely, often accompanying the anxiety about threats to themselves and/or others is a state of hypervigilance and jumpiness, causing overreaction to noises, the approach of others, or a touch on the arm (American Psychiatric Association, 2013). Many coerced women tell Loring during evaluations that they have difficulty concentrating, dwelling on the abuse as if it is happening all over again and struggling with intruding thoughts of the traumatic events (American Psychiatric Association, 2013). These flashbacks and intrusive thoughts are also found in many other trauma victims, such as prisoners of war and soldiers who have experienced the horrors of combat (American Psychiatric Association, 2013).

As discussed in chapter 2, van der Kolk (1994) has studied physiological changes accompanying trauma. He proposed that excessive stimulation of the CNS (central nervous system) when trauma occurs can actually cause permanent neuronal changes. These changes can hinder learning and stimulus discrimination; they do not depend on exposure to or reminders of the trauma to be expressed.

Many of the coerced need help in discovering the source of their feelings. Often they turn criticisms on themselves, believing what they hear about being worthless. (More about recovery and therapy will be discussed later.) During evaluations they have discussed a sense of helplessness, describing it in various ways: "I felt like a prisoner"; "I couldn't escape, like a captive"; "I was a hostage."

Lisa Felt Like a Hostage

Lisa was in her late teens when she met JJ, who was forty-eight years old. He wined and dined her, arranging for a private plane to fly them to the seashore for dinner and an evening stroll on the beach. More and more, he swept Lisa into his life, involving her in his efforts to sue and intimidate a number of people. He taught her how to do the necessary legal work and kept her busy all day and most evenings. His control became fanatical. She was to eat when he ordered, limit contact with her family, and comply with his demands, sexual and otherwise. Any contact with others would be under his close supervision. Her suggestions were put down and ridiculed, although he occasionally complimented her for following his orders. This emotional abuse reduced her to a sad and lonely person who was forced to rely on JJ for what little support she received. He insisted that she quit her job, and Lisa did so, succumbing to JJ's many threats to leave her and his warnings that she could not manage without him.

And when his legal maneuvers proved unsuccessful, JJ turned to dangerous plans of revenge. He involved Lisa in purchasing materials and, without her knowledge, used these materials to build a small explosive device, which he planted outside the front door of an enemy's home. When Lisa was arrested, along with JJ, she believed his insistence that the police had arrested the wrong person. Lisa could not bear to think that she had participated in terrorizing a family. She explained during the evaluation that she had felt like a hostage and never saw the danger for others.

I was so sure the police and FBI agents had the wrong man. I didn't think it could have been JJ. I believed whatever he said. I don't know why. The bombed family's fear was on TV. JJ laughed and said, "that was deserved." JJ's expression was so proud. I began wondering then. But it took a while to really believe it. I didn't want to scare anyone!

CAPTIVITY

One must see the possibility of escape before considering an attempt at it. But feeling helpless does not inspire such a vision of escape. In addition to helplessness, the coerced often describe feelings of fear and panic as well. Some of the coerced have grown up in homes where helplessness was like wallpaper that surrounded them. When women have witnessed physical and emotional abuse growing up, fear of rages and threats is not a new experience. Finding oneself in a situation similar to the past leads to less surprise than among those to whom it is new and different. Rather, the abuse seems like more of the same—more the norm.

Whenever the coercer is a person who has power in the community, such as an attorney or police officer, it becomes more difficult for the woman to seek and find effective help. The coerced can feel even more trapped because others may be hesitant to believe her or to cause trouble for her abuser. For example, when a coercer is a police officer, it can be difficult for a coerced woman to seek help and support from his fellow officers.

Deborah Sees No Choice

Married to a police officer, Deborah went out of her way not to upset him. Ray would go into rages, break lamps and furniture, and shove her roughly into walls and counters until she was bruised on her sides, arms, and legs. She worked as an investment counselor in a large firm. The director had attended the same college as Deborah, and they belonged to a sorority together. Ray insisted that Deborah inform him about good stocks to buy, although that was forbidden at the firm. He would give his brother money to buy investments that he learned about through confidential information he obtained from Deborah.

At one point Ray shoved Deborah and broke her arm; she called for help, but, when the police arrived, Ray talked them into giving him another chance. This happened again and again when she called police. Ray put all their bank accounts in his name so Deborah had no access to money, even her own paycheck. "I felt locked in," she said, "like I was in jail. He needed to approve where I went. I had to call him from where I went. If he didn't approve, I had to leave."

TORTURE AND BRAINWASHING

After capture for illegal behavior, coerced women often describe themselves as having been tortured, although they may not have been aware of this in the midst of their abuse, as they focused on safety issues. The coerced may be prevented from sleeping when coercers insist on talking or waking them up for various reasons. Other behaviors that many coerced have described as torturous during evaluations include being forced to endure their partner's dangerous driving, having medical treatment withheld, and being isolated from cherished family members. Being deprived of life goals and dreams and simple intimacy can also be painful experiences.

The coerced sometimes search for reasons to explain or understand the illegal behavior they have been caught up in. During their search for meaning, many describe coercion as an experience of being brainwashed. Biderman's Chart of Coercion (1973) has been used by Amnesty International to explain torture and brainwashing of prisoners and groups. Isolation is one factor in the chart; a group demands total obedience to the exclusion of previous supports and emotional ties. The demands of a group are similar to those of a coercive person who, as described in the chart, "deprives individual of social support, effectively rendering him unable to resist, makes individual dependent upon interrogator, develops an intense concern with self." The interrogator is like the coercive person who questions any disobedience and humiliates the person with public and/or private criticism and derogatory remarks, so much so that the coerced develops intense concern about succeeding with the assigned tasks and behaviors ordered.

A second process described in the chart is monopolization of perception. A church is used as an example, but the coercive process in the chart is similar to a coercive relationship in that "abusive groups insist on compliance with trivial demands related to all facets of life. They monitor members' appearances, criticize language. . . . They insist on precise schedules and routines, which may change and be contradictory from day to day or moment to moment, depending on the whims of group leaders."

A third part of Biderman's Chart of Coercion involves induced debility and exhaustion. This is often found in coercive relationships when the coerced describe exhaustion because of the tremendous demands of the coercer, sometimes including night time activities that did not allow enough sleep for work schedules the next day. Occasional indulgences are another part of the chart's described process of intimidation and power. Indulgences provide "motivation for compliance" (Biderman,

1973). If conflict develops, the leader might offer affection or support, thereby confusing the victims, who value the crumbs of affection. During evaluations, many coerced women report times of gentleness and encouragement. They feel grateful for these crumbs of support but wonder where they disappear to shortly afterward. Hungry and eager for love, the coerced have little ongoing joy or intimacy.

Devaluing the individual is also included in Biderman's coercion chart: The leader "creates fear of freedom and dependence upon captors, creates feelings of helplessness, develops lack of faith in individual capabilities" (Biderman, 1973). When the abusive leaders successfully get members to doubt the traits they most admire in themselves, "they begin to doubt everything else they have ever believed about themselves." (Biderman, 1973).

Information gained during evaluations indicate that self-doubt and despair are common among coerced who have been brainwashed. Some have low self-esteem and even dislike themselves. They often internalize the devaluing from the coercer and see themselves as worthless. This can be viewed as depression when the coerced are diagnosed by mental health professionals. It is unfortunate when the diagnosis does not take into account the psychosocial factors, such as coercion; this will be discussed later.

Bernice Seemed to Shrink

Married to a judge who demanded complete obedience at home, Bernice felt she lost her own personality, bit by bit, as she tried to please him. Bernice's efforts were aimed at avoiding his name-calling, shouting, slamming antiques against the wall, and threats to hurt her and their dog.

> I began to lose my zest for life. First, he insisted I give up my career. I was a French high school teacher. Then he controlled what I bought at market, who were my friends, even my opinions! When I obeyed his demands, he rewarded me with kindness and gifts. When I expressed my own ideas, he would humiliate me at parties or neighborhood gatherings. Mostly, he'd laugh at my ideas and call them "stupid" and "worthless." Sexually he ordered our activities, including watching pornography and visiting strip clubs. I felt like the real me had shrunk to what he wanted me to be. He told me how to think and what my opinions should be. I felt brainwashed.

TRAUMATIC BONDING

When the coercer is encouraging at one time, while threatening at others, traumatic bonding can be operating. In this special kind of bonding, the coerced is confused, wondering if her partner loves her or thinks she is worthless. Dutton and Painter (1993) described traumatic bonding where there is intermittent reinforcement—sometimes encouragement or warmth while, other times, violence or threats. Fear of harm weaves throughout the relationship and, if she leaves, then her sense of attachment and his begging and/or threats may propel her back. His promises to be kinder are hard to ignore when the woman's own self-esteem is at rock-bottom after continued criticism and degradation. And, when the violence is life-threatening, a coerced woman is caught in the conflict of loyalty versus fear and wish to escape.

Patsy's Traumatic Bonding

Patsy loved her boyfriend, Sam, but feared his gun-waving, constant taunting and teasing, and his insisting that she was not smart enough to complete graduate school. Patsy wanted to end her relationship with Sam. One evening, when she told him it was time to break off their relationship, he held a gun to Patsy's head and threatened to kill her, rather than lose her. Sam waved the gun around and held her captive in her apartment for three days, even when her absence from work resulted in a police visit and discovery of the situation. Yet, Sam would not give himself up. It was not until he was wounded by a police sniper that Patsy was rescued. To the surprise of the police and her family, Patsy expressed loyalty toward Sam. She described his depression and sense of loss when she announced their break-up. Patsy said she was so glad he hadn't hurt her and she did not want him punished. This situation is sometimes called the Stockholm Syndrome. As described in chapter 1, four Stockholm bank employees were held hostage at gunpoint in 1973. Upon their release they hugged and kissed their captors, declaring loyalty to them. They expressed a sense of gratitude for being allowed to live and survive an ordeal. In these situations, the captor identifies with the hostage taker, sometimes to the point of being understanding and sympathetic toward him.

Janice's Gratitude

When Larry took Janice out to his farm, he insisted that she spend the week with him. There were no telephones. He had "borrowed" her cell phone and declared it was buried out in the backyard, along with his own cell phone, to allow them a relaxing time away from the hectic world. Homes were quite a distance apart, and the car was locked in the garage. In fact, the house doors had key bolts and Janice was unable to go outside unless Larry unlocked the doors. Having met through a dating service, Janice found Larry attractive and interested in her, although she later discovered that information she shared with him was used to control and threaten her. Larry told her that he would hurt her beloved niece if she did not behave like a grateful guest for the week.

> I felt grateful he didn't hurt me. He talked about gruesome torture and murders he'd witnessed while in the army over in Iraq. When he cut the "vacation" short and we returned home in three days, I was so happy and relieved that I actually told the police, who were looking for me, that I was glad to be home and didn't want to press any charges.

SEPARATION FROM THE COERCER

There are important processes that initially prevent the coerced from leaving the coercer, even after the discovery of an illegal, sometimes dangerous and highly public crime.

1. Loss of self-identity
2. Low self-esteem
3. Trauma with confusion and terror
4. Fear of threats
5. Difficulty functioning

It is not easy, if even possible, for a woman to separate from a coercer and move on with life if the coercer has denigrated the woman's core values, identity, and important connections to others. Ripping one's self away from someone, no matter how cruelly coercive that person may be, is not likely to happen when the self is fractured. It takes a whole self and a sense of identity to detach, as will be described later in the transformation chapter.

Already low self-esteem cannot bear the weight of accusations about inadequacy and lack of worth. A continual barrage of negative labeling, put-downs, and other degradation leaves the woman without enough confidence to use her own perceptions and judgments with ease. Rather, her continual fear and vigilance leaves her drained and exhausted. Repeated threats and surveillance frighten and traumatize her. And she is confused and isolated, puzzled by the coercer's denials of his coercion and disregard for her needs and wishes. She also has difficulty functioning while coping with fear and anguish, creating dangerous conditions for jobs that depend on precision and concentration.

Among the coerced, health problems are not unusual due to the continual anxiety and discomfort. The coerced often report such ailments as stomach aches, headaches, poor or excessive appetites, sleep difficulties, breathing issues (it becomes hard to catch a breath or to stop hyperventilating), low energy, and poor concentration and focus. Later, during therapy, many see the symbolism of their aches ("My heart ached with such sadness") and actual pains ("My throat was sore a lot from holding back my crying").

6

Understanding Coercers in Relationships

Marianne Williamson (2002) wrote about the monsters in ourselves, how we do not understand that they live within us and how we mistakenly think we see them, and can slay them, outside in the world. She explained that the darkness in the world grows from darkness in our hearts.

INTERVIEWING COERCERS

Loring has spent many hours talking with coercive men. The two hundred-some men she has interviewed have lived throughout the United States, and about one-half reside in Georgia, South Carolina, and Alabama. There were three types of contacts with these men. For about half of them, his partner sought help with relationship problems. In those situations, the therapist's role involved exploring how each man could change his behavior toward a partner who chose to stay with him in a relationship. How could he adjust to—even support—changes in a transforming woman? Another purpose of interviews with coercive men involved seeking information that would help the coerced woman (his partner) who had been charged with participating in his crime. In addition, for some of the men charged with a crime, Loring's role was to evaluate each of them, and some were found to have been coercive in relationships.

It can be very difficult for family members, friends, and colleagues to accept the idea that some coerced women want to stay in a relationship with a coercer. Therapists often struggle with this choice, believing that life would be better for the coerced woman if she separated from him and became independent. And they may be right. For reasons discussed earlier, the coerced may be unwilling or unable to leave the coercer. During transformation of the woman (discussed later), two goals can be (1) helping the coercer change and (2) assisting him with acceptance and support of his transforming partner. Interacting in an activity with a coercer during interviews can be effective in learning about his history, connecting his past experiences with current behaviors, forming a relationship, and encouraging noncoercive behavior.

One example is Sam, a thirty-two-year-old coercer who forced his wife, Barbara, to visit strip bars, watch violent pornography, and participate in making pornography. He participated in a group that exchanged sex videos. One member of that group made a video that included a child, so all in the group, including spouses like Barbara, faced legal charges relating to child abuse.

In the course of Barbara's evaluation, Sam was willing to talk about his coercion. He acknowledged that he had made threats to abandon her and to take their child away by convincing protective services that she was a poor mother. Since Sam was a police officer, he worked with protective services on cases from time to time. Barbara believed that Sam's influence with the caseworkers would help him succeed in taking away her son.

The interview with Sam in jail helped identify his coercion of Barbara, giving more documentation to present in Barbara's case. It is important to listen to the coercer without judging and express appreciation for his sharing. In the case of Sam, he was open and responsive.

> I wanted to be a good husband. I wound up acting just like my father did. He didn't hit my mom. But he forced her to do what he wanted. He'd drag her into the bedroom. And leave the door cracked. I'd peek in. He left porn around on tables. I'd read the magazines and look at dirty pictures. I was mad a lot at my mom. She let him walk all over her. I guess I'm an angry guy. And I take a lot out on Barbara. I threaten her. I really use her sexually. And I'm mean to our dog.

During the plea before a judge, Barbara was sentenced to probation and Sam was sentenced to serve nine months in jail. He was released after five months and Barbara welcomed him home under certain conditions. While Loring's role as an evaluator was finished, Barbara asked for help and explained that she wanted to try remaining in the relationship. Loring saw them each several times separately to discuss the conditions that Barbara wanted. Sam was encouraged to get into individual psychotherapy and join an abuser group therapy program.

COERCERS IN THERAPY

Sam met with Loring several times to talk about his problems, although he sometimes insisted there was nothing wrong with him. Sam said he just lived in a repressive society. The intervention was framed as short-term help for Sam to support Barbara's growth, therapy, and transformation. Goals of the sessions were to be supportive and help motivate him to decrease coercive behavior. Sam did not want to follow through with a therapist for long-term therapy. Since the court mandated that he attend an abusers' group for a short period of time, he had no choice about that, other than to return to prison, which he did not want to do.

When Loring visited Sam's home, he was often watching football on television, shouting and ranting at players, criticizing and degrading them at every opportunity. They talked about the difference between the way he degraded the players and Barbara. Sam acknowledged there wasn't much of a difference. When reminded of his wish to be a good husband, better than his father had been, Sam realized the pattern he was repeating, and he expressed a wish to be more of a gentleman, which was a goal in his life encouraged by Loring. Respecting Barbara's feelings and not forcing her into behaviors was viewed (and described by Loring) as gentleman-like and his behavior changed slowly.

BATTERERS: TYPES AND PURPOSES

Donald Dutton (1995) has studied the psychological makeup of batterers. Dutton described different types of abusive men. Some men feel contrition for their violence, while others blame the woman without any compassion or empathy for her. Looking into the history of abusive men, Dutton has found that they often experienced abuse themselves. More than a learned behavior, he views their rage-fueled actions as a way of stabilizing themselves, just as other addictive behaviors can offer some relief (Dutton, 1995).

Dutton interpreted jealousy, so often seen among batterers, as a fear of abandonment, fear that the partner will leave for someone more sexually desirable (1995). Batterers project blame onto their partner for the very things that they themselves have done, seeing her as the cause of the problems and their discomfort.

Many batterers have experienced a shaming father, an ambivalent attachment with the mother, and violence in the home, all coming together to form a violence-prone man. Their fathers often gave them negative messages growing up, telling him that he was no good. Often there was also an absence of a constant, nourishing relationship with the mother, and parental violence was witnessed. Dutton pointed to the problems that batterers experience with communicating their intimate needs, finding it difficult to express their wishes, but becoming angry if the needs are not met. While coercers dictate orders and expect compliance, they are not able to ask for what they want in an intimate relationship, blaming the coerced for not meeting their needs (Dutton, 1995).

Gus Kaufman, cofounder of Men Stopping Violence, in Atlanta, Georgia, addressed the importance of understanding why men are violent and what will be effective intervention. Abusive men have usually been socialized by other men, taught they cannot have closeness with other men and that women, the only source of intimacy, must be controlled. Kaufman emphasized the controlling aspect of violence. When a woman wants to leave the relationship with a man socialized in this way, the man experiences this as losing control. He also may have other attachment deficits and trauma in his past (Gus Kaufman, personal communications, June 18, 2014).

Such men will use a variety of tactics to hold onto the woman. Some will engage in courtship behavior—apologizing for violence and offering gifts to the woman—in an effort to get her back under control. When women feel excluded in the relationship, men "drill into her that she is the reason for her own exclusion" (G. Kaufman, personal communications, June 18, 2014).

Kaufman believes that the anger witnessed among coercive men is actually a diversion from their need for systematic control: Abusive actions by men are often viewed as stemming from rage, but "men can do terrible things when not angry," when the quest for control is at the heart of their behavior. Kaufman views the men's behavior as an "exaggeration of what's normative: In culturally typical sex roles, women are raised to be submissive and men dominant—it's about being a man." The primary goal of most coercive men, according to Kaufman, is not simply to be oppressive, "but to obliterate the coerced as human beings, to make them into broken automatons" (G. Kaufman, personal communications, June 18, 2014).

COERCERS AS BATTERERS

Many coercers do not understand their own behavior. Some express sorrow that they have repeatedly emotionally, sexually, and/or physically hurt women they love. Others blame the woman as the source of all the problems. Some coercive men are also physical batterers, while others do not engage in physical abuse. In the cases presented here, the focus was on coercing a woman through threats and degradation into illegal or unwanted acts where subsequent humiliation and/or arrest and punishment were a likely outcome. While this occurs among some batterers, it does not for others.

COERCERS' JUSTIFICATIONS

When coercion into illegal behavior occurs, the man may have a police record of aggression and bullying. He often believes strongly in the righteousness and justification for the illegal act(s). Although he probably knows that the act is hurtful and/or illegal, his own needs trump this knowledge. With no regard for the values, self, or well-being of his partner, he drives and coerces her to further his goal. It is useful to explore how the illegal or unwanted act was presented to the coerced, because if he convinced her about his perceived righteousness of the act, he may have led her to believe that it was not illegal. Or he might have hidden the ultimate purpose of the multiple tasks he assigned to her.

Ted's "Sexual Antics"

After a speedy courtship and marriage, Ted insisted that Alice go with him to a neighborhood pub where back rooms were available for sexual behavior. He liked to pay for and watch sex between other couples in one of the back rooms. And he wanted Alice by his side. Three or four nights a week, he'd tell Alice, "Let's go have some sexual antics." When Alice told him she didn't want to go, Ted would threaten to call the principal where she taught school; he had forced Alice to take drugs once by spiking her drink, and he threatened to tell the principal that she used drugs. He also threatened to find out the date for drug testing at her school and said he would spike her food or drink the day before so she'd test positive for drug use: Alice taught at a high school with a no-drug policy, and she feared losing her job.

After a year of marriage, Ted continued to force Alice to go with him to the pub and to a few friends' sex parties where people switched partners for sexual acts. He then threatened Alice with the same revelation to the school for her alleged drug use, unless she took money from the school safe where school clubs' finances were stored. He said he'd expose her "taking drugs" unless she removed money from the school safe as he demanded. Since she was treasurer of two student clubs, Alice had access to the safe and these funds. She took cash on several occasions, and Ted used it to buy drugs. A hidden video camera showed them opening the safe and removing cash, and both were arrested. Ted agreed to talk with Loring when Alice was evaluated.

I feel bad I got her in trouble but she turned out to be disloyal. She promised she'd testify against me and she got probation. I got jail time. I write her letters and we'll get back together.

Ted wrote threatening letters to Alice, still determined to use the loss of her teaching job to scare her. But Alice had given all the information, including his threats to lie about Alice, to her principal, who put her on probation but let her remain on the school faculty.

EMOTIONALLY ABUSIVE COERCERS AS CONSULTANTS

Never meeting with both partners together, Loring has occasionally consulted with the man, challenging his views that his partner caused all of the problems and that he was faultless. She has explained to coercive emotionally abusive men that their criticisms, put-downs, and insistence on certain illegal behaviors would bother most people, so maybe that is what he should work on, rather than focusing only on blaming his partner. Some of the men have been willing to change, to modify negative remarks, or switch to a more positive and encouraging, supportive role. Some have reduced or eliminated coercive behaviors with continual reminding and firm limits set by a transforming woman. If a man is unwilling to change, this is something the woman must recognize before considering whether to stay in the relationship.

Loring never meets with the couple together if there was physical abuse in the relationship. This avoids the possibility of the man becoming enraged about something his partner did or did not say, possibly putting her in danger later. She has also met with partners separately when emotional abuse alone was present in order to avoid rages afterward over what occurred in the discussions.

Most of the changes among coerced and abused women are a result of their own growth and transformation in therapy. Enhanced self-esteem and confidence, willingness to connect with others, and growing accomplishments accompany transformative therapy, which will be discussed in a later chapter. Coerced women look for encouragement in various outlets, and the men should be encouraged to be supportive of whatever hobbies, connections, or careers the women pursue. Some men may purchase items their partner has indicated would be useful in her new adventures, such as a computer. In this sense, men might feel important in their limited participation, rather than feel a need to demean their partner in an effort to feel adequate themselves.

The woman should be encouraged to set limits with her partner, holding on to her own plans for growth and allowing his help when she asks for it. If life-threatening physical abuse is an issue, setting limits must be discussed with an eye toward her safety if the relationship is to continue.

If an emotionally abusive coercive man expresses a willingness to change, his first goals need to include supporting his partner's growth. Feeling like a coach and consultant, yet respecting her leading the way, the man can feel a sense of accomplishment. The man should also be willing to attend therapy or groups oriented to violence prevention, but that frequently does not happen without court-ordered attendance.

COERCIVE MEN FACING UNRELATED CHARGES

Loring has conducted numerous evaluations in which the man being evaluated had a history of coercion toward women although his current crime(s) did not involve this coercion. Learning about childhood abuse experienced by a man helps one to understand where his own violence comes from. Childhood abuse may also pertain when the man has not committed violence himself but may have been with another who did harm or kill someone. Then the questions include: Why would he be connected with a violent man? Was he hurt/controlled/coerced by this man, as he had been in his childhood?

Such was the case for Todd, who had been physically beaten on a daily basis by an alcoholic father while his mother, also an alcoholic, stood by and watched. Both parents were addicted to drugs. Todd was forced to engage in sexual activities with his sister, and his father threatened to kill him unless Todd obeyed. The father also earned money when he allowed two of his friends to engage in sexual activities with Todd.

As a young adult, Todd was with a man eighteen years older when they robbed a woman's house. The friend threw her to the floor and suffocated the woman, resulting in both being arrested and facing the death penalty. Todd had wanted to stop the murder.

> I couldn't believe that Mike was shoving the pillow in her face. I could hardly move. I kept seeing dad beating on mom. I did what Mike said to. He was like a father to me. And he'd beat me if I didn't.

Many states have laws in which both people participating in a robbery are held responsible for a victim's death, whether or not both actually participated in the murder. The information about Todd, which was documented by witnesses, police reports, and child service records, helped the court understand his life experiences. His coercion by and obedience to the older man was a mitigating factor in understanding his role during the tragic death of the woman. Mitigation is not meant to be an excuse for any event. Rather, it hopefully illuminates the whole picture, giving a context to behaviors.

STALKING AS A COERCIVE TACTIC

Coercers may use stalking to force a woman into certain types of behavior, for example, returning to a relationship. The Stalking Resource Center, National Center for Victims of Crime, defines stalking as "a pattern of repeated and unwanted attention, harassment, contact, or any other course of conduct directed at a specific person that would cause a reasonable person to feel fear." Stalking can include:

- Repeated, unwanted, intrusive, and frightening communications from the perpetrator by phone, mail, and/or e-mail.
- Repeatedly leaving or sending the victim unwanted items, presents, or flowers.
- Following or laying in wait for the victim at places such as home, school, work, or recreation place.
- Making direct or indirect threats to harm the victim, the victim's children, relatives, friends, or pets.
- Damaging or threatening to damage the victim's property.
- Harassing the victim through the Internet.
- Posting information or spreading rumors about the victim on the Internet, in a public place, or by word of mouth.
- Obtaining personal information about the victim by accessing public records, using Internet search services, hiring private investigators, going through the victim's garbage, following the victim, contacting victim's friends, family work, or neighbors, etc.

Stalking, often along with other behaviors, can be used to coerce someone into unwanted or illegal acts. These other behaviors can include rape, physical/sexual/emotional abuse, and threats to harm children, pets, partner, or parents. A coercer may utilize stalking for a number of purposes: to force someone into staying in/returning to a relationship, to frighten others and cause job loss or other consequences that put the victim into a dependent relationship with the stalker, to force the victim into complying with orders to join in illegal acts.

THE TIES THAT BIND

Many wonder why a woman would not leave a man who degrades and threatens her, possibly beats her, and may force her into unwanted illegal behavior and sexual activity. Lenore Walker (1984) described the cycle of violence that entraps many woman: the buildup of tension in a batterer, followed by an explosion, then followed by contrition. The contrition can come in different forms, like warmth, apologies, gifts, and promises to improve. These gifts and apologies can mean a great deal to a woman whose life has not contained more than occasional crumbs of warmth and appreciation. Loring has found during evaluations that, for some women, there is little, if any, contrition.

Additionally, when a man threatens terrible consequences, leaving is a dangerous proposition for a woman. Women can be harmed or killed during this precarious time of trying to leave the relationship.

As discussed earlier, Dutton (1995) described the fear of abandonment among batterers, suspecting signs of her leaving and jealous of others even when leaving is not on her mind. It is a sad problem. His ongoing jealousy and attempts to control her in order to keep her can drive an abused and coerced woman away.

In emotionally abusive relationships, there is often more continuous abuse than the model of tension buildup, explosion, and contrition. While there may be occasional gifts and appreciation, even sorrow at his own behavior, emotional abuse is ongoing with little relief for the woman (Loring, 1994).

One example is Tabatha, a fifty-five-year-old woman whose husband continually put her down and criticized her when they were alone or with others. Many had commented to her about his lack of respect and negativity toward her and she would dismiss them by explaining that he had been a foster child and abused by his parents. When she developed breast cancer, he expressed anger at the inconvenience of his having to take her to doctor appointments. He threatened to leave her if she did not cook meals and shop for food, and he expressed resentment at his having to hear about her discomfort during treatment. In front of her, he would complain to friends and family about her being ugly from hair loss during chemotherapy.

A nurse, overhearing his emotional abuse, asked Tabatha to consult with a therapist. Loring saw each of them and began therapy with Tabatha, occasionally seeing her husband, Bill, as a consultant. Having rarely experienced empathy and compassion during his childhood, Bill showed no caring toward his sick wife. He was referred to individual and group therapy, but he refused to do either. Tabatha was also raised in foster care after being removed from an abusive family. She wanted to continue therapy and to stay in the relationship with Bill.

Tabatha expressed her feeling that she had a tie with Bill because she understood his depression. She explained that she saw the pain behind his behavior. While working on her self-esteem, hopes in life, and talent with portrait painting, Tabatha joined an artist's group, painted portraits for which she was well paid, and volunteered in a nearby shelter for battered women. Tabatha also began to set limits for Bill, explaining that she would leave the room if he "didn't keep a civil tongue in his head." She demanded respect for her illness and recovery, telling him he was no longer to threaten to leave unless she performed certain acts, like cooking when sick. When Bill said he didn't know how to do all of this, she suggested he attend a men's group at the shelter—if he wanted to keep their relationship. He attended the group.

> I felt very connected with Bill and thought I didn't mind his being mean to me. I understood where it came from. But I decided I deserved more in life. I don't get it all from him. But I get a lot more. And my art leads to many friendships.

Bill continued to make efforts to be supportive, like buying the art supplies that she requested. He finally agreed to get therapy for his own depression. Loring talked with him about his lack of empathy and compassion and wondered how he could learn those skills. He began reading books about these topics and made efforts to practice more compassion.

Breaking the ties that bind can mean increasing the woman's other ties. As explained earlier, when safety is an issue, then expanding freedom for a coerced woman must be done carefully, if at all. The question of whether she will be safe must be asked; this same question should be asked regarding the therapist, who could be viewed by the coercer as encouraging abandonment. When safety is not an issue, the man has a choice whether to leave or stay with her and show more respect and support.

Tabatha was flooded with praise for her portraits, and she was able to separate more from Bill's emotional abuse and occasional coercion: The coercion had grown from threatening to leave her if she did not cook to demanding that she take things he wanted from hospital rooms while being treated, such as boxes of vinyl gloves and Kleenex boxes. While not big items, Bill would insist that she bring him several after each doctor's visit. The penalty for disobeying was that he would be cold and ignore her. Frightened of abandonment herself, Tabatha obeyed his orders until sometime after she began therapy. She then told him she would not do it and, if he became cold and ignored her, she would volunteer at the shelter or go up to the attic where she had built a studio for her painting.

If a coercive man becomes angry with the woman's growing self-esteem, afraid she will abandon him, there needs to be care that he does not physically harm her, even if the relationship has been solely emotionally abusive. Attention needs to be paid to his feelings in order to keep an ongoing focus on the woman's safety. Safety rules must be clear. Tabatha attended a battered woman's group where this was a priority. Bill, in his violence prevention group, was supported in taking responsibility for his own behavior and never throwing anything (which he had done in the past) or threatening her.

ABUSE AS A WAY OF LIFE

For many men who abuse, violence has always been a way of life. Dutton (1995) has described these men becoming addicted to violence as a means of gaining a sense of relief. The absence of problem-solving and communication skills is clearly present among many of these men, which is why violence prevention groups are so valuable in learning skills and acceptance of responsibility.

Many coerced women understand the pain from which their partners operate. As with Tabatha, Bill's depression and fear of loss aroused her sympathy, another factor that tied her to him. Yet, if a woman is coerced into stealing, this can lead to the loss of her self-respect and belief in herself. Tabatha experienced humiliation when stealing from those who were helping her regain health. Unfortunately, Bill had a lack of awareness or caring about the impact of his demands and threats. Violation of the woman's values is an additional type of coercive violence that was experienced by Tabatha.

I felt like dirt to take those things from the doctor's office. But I was scared of Bill ignoring me or leaving home for a time. I feel so much better now. If he ignores me, I have other friends now and my studio. When I paint, I come alive.

7

The Coercive Process
Overt and Covert Emotional Abuse

Jean Baker Miller (1988) describes isolation as terrifying and destructive, leading to desperate loneliness and feelings of being locked out of human connection. People who see no possibility of connection may believe the reason for their exclusion lies within themselves; feeling powerless and helpless, many will do almost anything to escape isolation.

OUT IN THE OPEN: OVERT EMOTIONAL ABUSE

Emotional abuse drives coercion, where feelings of isolation are overwhelming. There are different styles of emotional abuse. Some are out in the open, overt, and direct: The coercer issues orders to a woman, whether in public or at home. These orders are degrading and spoken harshly, without consideration for the woman's wishes, feelings, safety, or dignity. Many people, both in and out of the family, notice this bullying behavior, and are puzzled that their advice to leave the abuser is ineffective. It is hard for many to understand how a woman can lose so much of herself that independence becomes unimaginable.

Bev Felt Captive

Bev said that she had never been in a real jail before, but Ben's rules and consequences felt like a prison.

> My mother said Ben ruled me with an iron hand. There were rules, his of course, about when we woke up, went to sleep, shopped—the groceries were

all of his own picking. It's hard to explain, but—if I didn't obey—he'd first sulk, then go in a different room, and finally leave the house for days on end, without calling or returning for his asthma inhaler. I'd worry and be afraid to go out, because one time I saw him watching from across the street. When I went outside, he wasn't there, like he was hiding. I called and called but he never came out from wherever he was. This happened a few times and I learned it was easier to do what he said than to worry. Once, when I saw Ben watching me from across the street, I went out and he wasn't there, so I asked my neighbor who was cutting grass and he told me he'd seen Ben standing on the sidewalk in front of his house. The reason I asked was that Ben always denied having watched me.

COVERT EMOTIONAL ABUSE

Hidden and disguised, this subtle form of emotional abuse can easily go unrecognized by others who have not been trained in the language of covert coercion. But the coerced are alert to this language, for example, symbolic gestures like the coercer rubbing his throat to signal a threat of choking.

Denial

Denial by the coercer is a powerful form of covert emotional abuse. In Bev's situation above, Ben denied that he was anywhere nearby, so Bev thought she was imagining his surveillance. These more subtle, hidden styles of coercion may not be evident to others or even to the woman herself. The coercer insists he never said this or that, even when others had overheard him. Or he may go the opposite way of denying the truth, claiming that he gave an order that she did not hear or failed to obey. The coercer thus fosters self-doubt in the coerced, whose supposed failure to listen or obey becomes the focus of his attention.

Projection

The coerced get blamed for a lot, including all the anxiety, discomfort, and fear that plagues the relationship. Instead of saying, "I feel uncomfortable when you talk with that good-looking man," the coercer may accuse his partner of flirting, intending to leave him, purposefully causing him anxiety, or having an affair with this stranger. When she tries to assure him that she has no interest in anyone else, no plans to leave him, no intention to cause him discomfort, the coercer refuses to reconsider his view and insists that his discomfort and anxiety are caused by the coerced. Meanwhile, any refusal or inability to obey the coercer's strict orders is met with accusations of disloyalty, disrespect, and/or a lack of love for him. He sees her as inconsiderate and unloving, yet her own wishes and values are never considered. Desperate, confused, and lonely, the coerced feels isolated from the partner as well as from herself, since she is accused of deeds of which she was not even aware.

Labeling

Labeling is part of covert emotional abuse. In intimate coercion, it is common for the coerced to be labeled as inadequate in areas that she values, for example as a poor mother; a bad wife; or simply unattractive, stupid, and worthless. These negative labels are used to compel the coerced to follow the orders: If you weren't such a bad wife, you would do what I have asked.

Gwen's Acceptance

Gwen believed her live-in boyfriend when he called her "stupid" and said she would never succeed because of her being so "timid." But, Wayne assured her, he would guide her toward braver and wiser behavior. So Wayne ordered her life and gave her directions. Gwen tried to follow his advice, which included dropping out of community college and getting a job at the check-in desk at a hotel. Her family and friends found her becoming less confident and more anxious. And they were shocked when Gwen was accused of stealing money from a gift shop in the hotel. Her lawyer asked for an evaluation when he was told that Wayne was ordering and controlling Gwen while she was in jail. Wayne was writing her long letters with instructions about what to say and how to act.

During the psychosocial evaluation, Gwen said that she was glad to be arrested because she was now freer than she had been in a long time.

> The worst of it was, I believed the things he called me—stupid, flirtatious, without sexuality, ugly. He'd repeat it over and over until I saw those things when I looked in the mirror. I feel so free. And I don't read his letters, just give them to the sergeant.

Discounting

To discount another is to cast doubt on her thoughts, feelings, or actions. When a coercer tells his partner that her idea is silly or uninformed, it is an attempt to discredit her perception, which he views as unimportant and worthless, certainly not valuable or meaningful. Discounting is part of intimate coercion where the coerced gets repeated messages that she has nothing important to contribute. By discounting her ideas, the coercer paints them as less important than his ideas and not as valuable or worth talking about. Rather, the coercer insists that his thoughts are the only ones worth considering, especially when these thoughts are translated into orders to be followed.

Tammy's Loss of Confidence

Tammy, a banker who enjoyed writing poetry, had been an honor student in college and earned high grades in graduate school. She applied for a job in a large city bank and was excited when she was hired. To her surprise, her boyfriend, Sandy, expressed unhappiness with her success. When she told him about training at the bank and the colleagues she liked, Sandy was quick to say that the training for her new executive position was not thorough or demanding.

> He told me my ideas for being a banking executive were not modern, were old fashion. He said people in positions under me would not think my ideas were important. I spoke during training on the importance of encouraging the whole team in ways that made them feel their contributions were valuable. When I told Sandy about the trainer's enthusiasm for what I had said, Sandy said he wasn't an experienced trainer because my idea was not feasible and would take too much time. I began to believe I wasn't fit for the job. I felt really discouraged. And Sandy would order me around like telling me when to leave for work and when to have sex.

Negation

Negating another's ideas is like erasing all that someone has written on a blackboard. Rather than suggesting that a feeling is unimportant, like in discounting, the actual existence of that feeling is erased during negation. The feeling or thought does not exist, according to the coercer. If the coerced says she feels frightened to follow an order, the coercer may reply, "No, you don't feel frightened. No one feels frightened in this situation."

And the coerced does not experience negation as a one-time reply. Rather, there are continuous negations and discounts, as well as labeling, denial, and projection (Loring, 1994). With covert emotional abuse, the extent to which a coercer is belittling the coerced is rarely clear to observers, due to the hidden nature of the abuse. Even the coerced may not see the hidden discounts and negations for what they are, and thus confusion is a common reaction. Low self-esteem and discouragement in the coerced often accompany the degradation: She is told she is unimportant, doomed to fail, uninteresting, even unkind; internalizing this message, she begins to believe in her lack of worth, which makes her more vulnerable to coercion.

Risks of Covert Emotional Abuse

For women subjected to covert emotional abuse, feelings of discouragement, despair, anguish, and sadness can become overwhelming and thus dangerous. During evaluations or therapy with coerced people, it is important to check: Are they experiencing thoughts about harming or killing themselves? This is called suicidal ideation in the mental health field. They should be asked if they are self-medicating with drugs or alcohol, and if these are being used while driving or working in a field that demands concentration and precision. If the coerced feels like her sense of self is lost, self-harm may be a cry for help, especially if she is unable to understand the loss. And, as has been discussed previously, some coerced women may be pressured by their partners into taking such illegal drugs as cocaine, crack, marijuana, and methamphetamine.

Frances Seeks Help for Sadness

Frances, unsure what was causing her sadness, called a counselor for an appointment. Feeling empty and desperate, she poured out her experiences, as well as how she feared her boyfriend, Danny, when he became angry and sullen. He was jealous of her work, her parents, even their dog. Danny accused Frances of being more affectionate with others than with him. He discounted and negated her feelings and accused her of having affairs and disrespecting him. Danny labeled her as stupid and mean. Frances felt confused and hopeless.

> And when I went for counseling, my counselor thought I was depressed and she was right. But we didn't discuss why and how I could get better. I felt disappointed that I didn't explain better.

It is a challenge for therapists and others who are intervening to identify those who experience covert emotional abuse when many of the coerced are not aware of the extent or impact of the abuse and coercion they are suffering under. The coerced often do not know why they experience feelings of isolation and loneliness. A therapist who is knowledgeable about power, control, isolation, and coercion can help coerced women recognize the pattern and understand the situation they are in.

8

Evaluation of Coercion

T. S. Eliot (1943) wrote about exploring and searching in our lives, only to arrive after each exploration back at our starting point, at last coming to know that point for the first time. Understanding the coerced involves knowing their starting points: possible early abuse, coercion, control, and loss of hope.

IDENTIFYING COERCION

When interviewing clients or patients, health and mental health professionals should always include questions that explore whether someone is experiencing physical, emotional, or sexual abuse or coercion. Coercion can be discovered in hospital emergency room interviews, during routine medical checkups, and in psychotherapy. Direct caring and concerned questions can help uncover information about abuse and coercion. Some important questions to ask are:

1. Have you been afraid for your own or a loved one's safety?
2. Are you frightened about anyone harming your pet or an animal?
3. Do you ever feel forced into doing things you don't want to do?
4. Are you experiencing someone putting you down, calling you names?
5. Do you feel humiliated and degraded in your intimate relationship?
6. Are you kept away from family and friends?
7. Does someone take over your money and control it?

8. Are you controlled by anyone in terms of your time or any other way?
9. Do you hear threats that frighten you?
10. Do these threats aim at getting you to do things?
11. What threats or behaviors are most frightening to you?
12. Do you ever resist these threats or resist obeying orders?
13. How do you resist?
14. What happens after you resist?
15. How do you cope with frightening threats or behavior?
16. What supports do you have to cope with this?
17. How does all of this impact you?
18. How is your functioning affected?
19. Do you have a job that requires attention and focus?
20. Is your concentration and ability to work affected by all of this?
21. Is your driving affected by all of this?
22. Is your health affected by all of this?
23. Do you think that others are at risk because of what you experience?

There certainly could be additional questions and discussion about the answers. The goal is to locate those experiencing abuse and coercion in time to protect them from participating in unwanted and/or illegal behavior. For those not involved in illegal behavior, the need is to provide help when they are coerced into behaviors that are uncomfortable, painful, or betray their values and dreams in life. Dutton, Goodman, and Schmidt's coercive control research article (2006) is an excellent resource for considering additional interview questions about coercion.

Trauma from coercion is not based on a single assault. Rather, the concept of complex trauma as outlined by Herman (1997) best describes the nature of coercion where the abusive incidents or threats are multiple and ongoing. During some evaluations, it becomes evident that the coercer's threats are used to convince the coerced that harm is imminent, like the coercer telling stories about his past violence.

COLLECTING INFORMATION

Attorneys may ask professionals to evaluate for the possibility of coercion after someone's arrest for participating in an illegal act. There are crucial areas to be explored during such evaluations. It is necessary to talk with the woman, herself, whether she is incarcerated or out of jail on bond, and interviewing the coercer can be helpful if it is possible. When there are charges against him as well, his attorney may not want him speaking with anyone, but it never hurts to ask. There have been times when the coercer has been willing to talk with Loring and this has helped with the collection of information about the relationship and provided direction in the search for whether or not coercion was operating at the time of the incident or crime.

After an interview with someone who may or may not have been coerced, one approach is to create a "wish list" to share with attorneys. This list may contain names of people who could be interviewed as collateral witnesses, meaning they might provide more information about the woman's history, relationship to the coercer, and behavior during the incident. Some of these collateral witnesses may have suffered injuries or losses as a result of the coercer's behavior. The wish list can include documents to review. Sometimes, an attorney or someone designated by the attorney will obtain them. In other cases, the expert might request information and documents such as hospital and education records, police reports, doctor's visits, and therapy charts.

Obtaining documents usually involves a form that the woman signs allowing the health facility to release records. However, on a death penalty case, there is often a mitigation specialist who interviews witnesses and obtains documents before a coercion, abuse, and/or trauma evaluator is even brought onboard as a possible expert witness. Of course, if no coercion, abuse, or trauma is found by the evaluator, it is unlikely that the evaluator will be used as an expert witness.

TRAUMA INFORMATION

It is important to note that evaluation is not therapy: Collecting and organizing information, analyzing behavior and interaction, is not intended to involve therapeutic intervention, which is a separate process.

Threats to harm the woman and those dearest to her are often fierce and frequent during coercion. Given this environment, trauma is common among the coerced and exploring trauma symptoms is part of coercion evaluation: How does the woman sleep and what fears interfere? Does she reexperience terrifying situations over and over, seeing them as if they are happening when they are actually in the past?

Mental health professionals differ in the way they evaluate individuals for trauma. Some differences grow from professional training and specialties: Psychiatrists and counselors often interview clients to assess and diagnose; many psychologists use various psychological tests to search for trauma symptoms; clinical social workers, clinical sociologists, and some additional professionals often include interviews not only with a client, but also with family members and others who have witnessed life events.

Historical information is important to assess for trauma. What traumatic event(s) has the person experienced at which developmental stages of life? One or more traumatic events during childhood can lead to trauma symptoms continuing into adulthood.

During evaluations for possible trauma and coercion, Loring may use trauma tools like the Clinician-Administered PTSD Scale (CAPS). There are other similar tools that reveal the presence or absence of trauma symptoms. These tools can be used by mental health professionals from various professional backgrounds. It is important to understand what, if any, trauma symptoms the person has experienced, and whether these symptoms affected behaviors at the time of an illegal incident.

As suggested, a person's trauma can be discovered by getting a social history of her life. It is valuable for interviews with those possibly coerced to include questions about her history such as the following:

1. What frightening experiences has the woman experienced and at which ages?
2. Are there repetitions of fearful experiences?
3. How have they impacted her life?
4. Were there environmental supports that helped her?
5. Were there supportive people and how did they help?
6. How was she affected by such factors as poverty and dangerous neighborhoods?
7. What were her school experiences?
8. Was she previously seen by mental health professionals?
9. What were the diagnoses and impressions?
10. Was counseling provided and was it helpful?
11. Was she bullied, raped, or stalked? When and how and with what outcome?
12. Were there people who believed and supported her?
13. What were the intimate relations like in her home growing up?
14. How was she treated by parents, siblings, relatives, neighbors, babysitters?
15. What types of abuse did she witness, including animal abuse?
16. Did she witness adult intimate relationships with abuse? What types?
17. What was her role in the above situation (protector, calling for help, etc.)?
18. What health issues and accidents did she experience in life?
19. Are there available psychotherapy notes, health/hospital records, and educational records?
20. Has she had previous legal problems?
21. Has anyone forced her into unwanted and/or illegal behaviors?

22. Has she been threatened? How and what was the outcome?
23. If so, how did/does she handle it?
24. Was bullying part of her history?
25. Did she experience acts of violence growing up and/or in previous relationships?

All of these areas are important to discuss with the woman. She can provide contact information for collateral witnesses—others with knowledge about her life/relationships.

WHEN COERCION IS IMPORTANT

If an attorney suspects abuse and coercion when a woman has been accused of illegal behavior along with her partner, an expert may be called upon to evaluate the individual. These crimes can include fraud, robbery, theft, driving violations, kidnapping, drugs, child abuse, assault, murder, and bombings, among others. At first, both the woman and her partner may be accused without any separation of responsibility (who played what part in the crime). But if a woman has experienced coercion, her role in the illegal incident can be understood in a different light. Coercion may be a mitigating factor when sentencing is considered in both state and federal courts.

Sometimes the expert testifies in front of a jury. Other times there is no jury and a judge makes the determination of punishment, as in Maria's case, which follows. In this case, the defense lawyer and the district attorney both acknowledged that Maria was guilty, but they could not agree about her sentence. So they asked the judge to decide, bringing to him a plea of guilty and presenting both sides. The district attorney wanted Maria to have a jail sentence, while the defense lawyer asked for probation with no jail time.

Maria

Maria, a thirty-two-year-old administrative assistant in an automotive store, was accused of theft when merchandise began disappearing during hours that she worked late, after all of the other employees had left the store. When questioned by the manager, Maria appeared nervous and cried, rather than denying any involvement. Police were called, and she demonstrated the same anxious behavior. After Maria was arrested, her home was searched and some of the stolen items were found.

Her boyfriend, Lewis, disappeared, and only later were the police able to locate and arrest him. A detective discovered that he had been selling items stolen from the store. Their seven-year-old daughter, Mia, was taken into foster care. Both the police and Maria's attorney suspected coercion. When Maria and her boyfriend were both in the courtroom together for a hearing, Maria hid first behind a police officer and then, grabbing her lawyer's jacket, hid behind him, trying to avoid Lewis's angry glares and fist-shaking gestures. Many in the courtroom saw him shake his fist at her until a court deputy told him to stop. Maria began shaking and crying. Later, during a psychosocial evaluation, she described her fear. "When he shook his fist, I almost fainted. I just knew he'd hurt our daughter Mia. That was what he'd do before hurting her—shake his fist."

AREAS FOR EXPLORATION

There are many areas for exploration when evaluating a person who may or may not have been coerced during her participation in a crime.

1. What kinds of experiences could have led to her present situation?
2. Have there been abusive experiences during her life that would add understanding to the incident for which she is now in trouble?
3. If she is in a relationship with her partner-in-crime, are there patterns of coercion?
4. What kinds of abuse in that relationship could help understand her participation in the crime?
5. If she has been experiencing trauma, what kind of trauma and how does it relate to her role in the crime?
6. Are there repeated threats and how do they relate to the crime?
7. Has she believed that threats will be carried out if she does not obey orders?
8. What does all this have to do with the unwanted and/or illegal behavior?
9. Was there coercion at the time of a crime?
10. Is she still being coerced after the arrest?
11. What is her current emotional state?

When someone who may have been coerced is interviewed, she can be asked to sign "release forms" that will allow interviews with collateral witnesses, which may shed light on aspects of her life and her possible participation in unwanted behavior and/or an illegal incident. For example, her previous therapists would need a release to discuss her history, their impressions and diagnoses. There are various collateral witnesses who are important to seek out, such as parents and siblings, friends and neighbors, previous therapists, people related to her partner or his friends, doctors and others who have treated the woman and her partner including her own medical and mental health records and the partner's (if possible), witnesses to the incident, anyone else participating in the crime, and crime victims.

More collateral witnesses and documents can be added and explored as the evaluation continues. Some records are not easily obtainable, for example, the partner's medical records, but it can be helpful to review records that reveal mental health issues of the coercer, who may give permission in some cases.

ORGANIZING INFORMATION

The expert does not necessarily write a report in each case. In the interest of time, the focus may be on interviewing the woman and collateral witnesses, as well as obtaining/reviewing documents. In other situations, the lawyer may want a report to use when considering a plea bargain. In a plea, the lawyers can suggest a punishment to the judge. Or, after reviewing a report and other information, the attorneys may ask the judge to determine the sentence, as was the case with Maria. Whether or not a report is requested, the information needs to be organized in some way to explain the behavior.

Was coercion present? If so, then what kind and how did this coercion influence the woman's actions? The information gathered can be used to create charts that a jury and/or judge can examine in the courtroom. These charts can be held by the expert or projected onto an overhead screen. The charts demonstrate important events in a woman's life. These charts will be described later in this chapter. They can include a trauma timeline, a life or relationship history chart, and/or a genogram (family diagram). The evaluator should select charts, depending on what is helpful in explaining a case.

PSYCHOSOCIAL EVALUATIONS

This section will outline psychosocial evaluations. The structure is as follows: A component of the psychosocial evaluation is introduced, followed by a summary of a case and a quote from the coerced, and then a selection from her psychosocial evaluation to place her feelings and experiences into a forensic context.

A psychosocial evaluation, as the name implies, examines the person in her social context, including family, educational, and social factors. The sections included in an evaluation are an introduction, history, history of current and previous relationships, details of the incident, diagnosis and/ or the impact of diagnosis on the incident, and (sometimes) recommendations. Other information such as a life history chart, a trauma chart, and/ or a genogram may supplement the evaluation.

These evaluations involve more than diagnoses. Explanations focus on the impact of possible coercion and trauma on illegal behavior and post-incident behavior (behavior after the crime). When recommendations are included, they involve the use of therapeutic interventions and other resources to promote growth and change.

It should be noted that a diagnosis in a psychosocial evaluation may be a specific diagnosis, or it may consist primarily of diagnosed symptoms, such as sadness or depressive withdrawal, fearfulness or traumatic terror, rather than an actual diagnostic term. The goal is to relate these symptoms/diagnoses to behaviors that were present during an incident if that is possible. Previous diagnoses or observations about symptoms are often useful in understanding a person. The psychosocial evaluation is an information-gathering effort in order to organize and present a clear picture of a person to the court. The evaluator should have experience and training in the areas of trauma, abuse, family development, social factors that help shape a personality, and diagnoses in the DSM-V, as well as a willingness to listen without being judgmental.

Psychosocial Evaluation: Introduction

It is sometimes valuable for the evaluator to include an introduction at the beginning of a psychosocial evaluation. A curriculum vitae (CV) may be made available to document the evaluator's education, training, qualifications in the areas being evaluated, and accomplishments. The introduction may also include the locations of meetings (jail, home, etc.) as well as the length of time and the date of each interview, and the client's appearance and mood in the interviews. Lists of collateral witnesses interviewed and documents reviewed (possibly police reports and witness statements) may also be included. Further, the means of evaluating trauma symptoms are included, such as CAPS or whatever tools may be utilized by the evaluator.

It has been mentioned previously that evaluation is not therapy. Therefore it is important to inform the woman that she does not have confidentiality while answering questions during an evaluation. Some evaluators use a release form, asking the woman to sign and indicate her understanding that information may be shared in reports and/or during court proceedings. As noted earlier, identifying information is disguised in the psychosocial evaluations included throughout this book. The evaluations discussed here may have been submitted to the court prior to a trial, used for a plea bargain decision, presented in court for the judge to consider during sentencing, or not used at all for a variety of reasons.

Andrea's Lawyer Requested an Evaluation

Andrea had been arrested and her lawyer asked for an evaluation. The day care center for her two-year-old son, Pete, had reported to child protective services and the police that Pete was bruised. At the hospital, the child's examination revealed a broken arm. Both Andrea and her boyfriend, Danny, were arrested. Pete was kept in a foster home while Andrea and Danny were evaluated as caregivers. Andrea's parents put up the money to bail her out of jail; Danny remained incarcerated.

Danny was willing to talk to Loring while his lawyer was present. (The attorney protected Danny from saying anything that could be used against him in court.) Danny admitted that he had a "bad temper" and described having trouble with the toddler, who would not obey and had tantrums, especially at bedtime. Loring commented that some children who avoid bedtime with stubbornness and temper tantrums may be having problems with anxiety. Danny expressed surprise. Andrea and Danny were both twenty-three years old and seemed to know little about child development and care.

In a separate discussion, Andrea explained that Danny would put their son to bed, insisting that she stay in the living room and let there be "male bonding." But, when their son refused to go to sleep, Danny would yell and force Pete to stay in the bed. If Andrea walked down the hall to help, Danny would get even angrier and shove Pete against the wall.

Charges against Andrea included "failure to protect," while Danny was charged with cruelty to children. Andrea kept in touch with her son, who was allowed to talk on the telephone with her daily; she also had supervised visits with him twice a week.

> I was afraid to call the police. Danny said he'd tell them I was such a poor mother that I'd made bruises on Pete. I didn't. He told me so much how bad a mother I was. I really believed it. And I was nervous all the time that I'd hurt my son. But I never did.

Loring created a "wish list" of collateral witnesses and began interviews and requested documents to review. Below is a section of Andrea's psychosocial evaluation. Sometimes the person's birthdate is included underneath the name. In this introduction, the context is laid out for the information that follows. As explained previously, the term *psychosocial* is used because of the evaluation's social context. More than a diagnosis of an individual, there is a family, cultural, and historical perspective.

It is not always necessary to identify the roles of the collateral witnesses interviewed (mother, father, etc.) when listing them in the psychosocial evaluation. Whether or not to list their roles or relationships is decided by the evaluator, who will also select a way to refer to the client: Mrs., Ms., Mr., or the first name throughout the psychosocial evaluation.

Psychosocial Evaluation
Andrea Kevinson
DOB: 4/6/78

This evaluator, a licensed clinical social worker and clinical sociologist, specializes in the areas of abuse, trauma, and coercion (please see CV). Ms. Kevinson was interviewed on the following three dates: July 9, 14, and 21, 2011. Each interview lasted approximately three hours for a total of nine interview hours. The first two interviews occurred at the Jackson County Jail and the third interview took place at her home after release from jail. The following collateral witnesses were interviewed: Mr. Sam Kevinson and Ms. Emma Kevinson (her mother and father); Danny Ison Jr. (her boyfriend and the codefendant); Pete Kevinson (her seven-year-old son) and his pediatrician, Dr. Pason; Mr. and Mrs. Alan Simpson (her neighbors); social worker Jess Harden (her therapist); Mr. and Mrs. Danny Ison (Danny's mother and father); and Janice Smother and Annie Wyatt (young Pete's teacher and teacher's aide).

Documents reviewed included Pete's hospital records from Jackson Health Center, Jackson Police Department Incident Reports on June 4, 2011, Danny Ison's previous family violence police reports, witness statements to the Jackson Police Department (June 4, 2011), as well as police statements of Andrea Kevinson and Danny Ison Jr.

While interviewing Andrea Kevinson, the Clinician-Administered PTSD Scale (CAPS) was used. It was explained to her that the interviews were not confidential. She indicated that she understood.

Her mood was anxious and depressed. She expressed sadness about her son's broken arm and about missing him. She asked for information about his well-being. By the time of our last interview, she had visited her son. Ms. Kevinson told this evaluator that Mr. Ison had been sending her threatening notes in jail and at home. She gave these notes to her lawyer.

Psychosocial Evaluation: History

It can be challenging to learn about historical information without being judgmental. For each evaluator, the vulnerabilities are different: Among many evaluators, it is hard to hear details about animal or child abuse. Evaluators may need to watch their own trauma levels when hearing about these types of abuses and viewing images of wounds or autopsy pictures. Therefore, it is important that those doing evaluations have good support systems themselves. Learning the background about horrible historical acts of abuse and torturous treatment can take a toll, leading to a sense of trauma and grief. Herman's (1997) description of the trauma that therapists can experience when helping abused people would apply to evaluators as well.

One purpose of an evaluation is to gain an understanding of what drives a person to behave in certain ways. While not excusing behaviors, learning about life history can provide information about why behaviors are adopted. Below is Ellen's history.

Ellen's History of Survival

Ellen's lawyer requested an evaluation after she was arrested and charged with reckless endangerment of another and disobeying a police officer. She had been riding in the passenger seat of a car when Billy, her boyfriend, struck a pedestrian. Although a police officer had rushed out of a restaurant and shouted at the car to stop, Billy continued to drive. A police chase ensued and Billy and Ellen were eventually pulled over. After the police took them from the car, Ellen refused to talk with them or give any information. One police officer at the scene later explained that Ellen showed him a picture of her dog, but would not talk with him. He described her as crying, shaking, and looking fearfully at Billy. Later, during the psychosocial evaluation, Ellen shared the reason for her silence.

> Billy told me he'd kill my dog when he got out on bail if I talked to the police. He knows how to get out on bail. He's been arrested before and got out. He said the only way I could save my dog was to be quiet, completely silent. So I did. I had been screaming at him to slow down, but he raced right through that intersection and hit the woman. I hope she's OK. I couldn't help but show the police a picture of Penny, my little dog.

> Psychosocial Evaluation
> Ellen Grant
> History

Ellen was born in Illinois and moved continually; her father was a career army officer. Ellen grew up with a mother, father, and two brothers. Frightened of her father Larry, she would hide from him when he returned home from work intoxicated. Sometimes she'd hide under a bed, waiting for him to pass out. Other times, the mother, Mabry Grant, described flinging open the front door and shouting for the children to run to safety.

But they did not always find safety. On one occasion, her father demanded to know what a brother had done to make Ellen cry. She was fearful of telling her father, but the brother, Tony, confessed to having teased her. Larry placed Tony's hand on the bannister of the outside porch and crashed his (father's) leg down upon the extended arm of her brother, breaking it. Both Ellen and her mother recalled this event. In another incident, Larry forced fourteen-year-old Ellen to come into the bathroom and watch as thirteen-year-old Tony was placed naked in a bathtub, followed by her father taking a scissors and cutting off all of Tony's hair.

Ellen also witnessed her father meeting Tony as he came home from school. When Tony stepped off the school bus, the father beat him until he was bloody and bruised. Ellen was made to watch while her father kicked Tony, over and over. Ellen described wondering what she could do to help her brother; she felt helpless. Police arrested her father after this school bus incident and Tony was treated at the hospital. Her mother also recalls this, insisting that the father was a good provider and that she regrets some things in the past when she failed to protect her children.

Ellen shook and cried during the evaluation interview, describing her father holding a gun to each of the children's heads, telling them that he could kill them anytime. Ellen remembers each of her brothers aiming a gun at her father on different occasions. She reports growing up terrified and often feeling helpless.

Once her father took her cocker spaniel dog away to the woods out back of their house. He had a gun in his hand and the family heard several shots. When he returned to the house, the dog, Scampi, was not with him. She never saw Scampi again.

When her father would order Ellen, at age fourteen, to drive him to the bar, he would insist that she drink alcohol with him. He'd threaten that she had better drive well on the way home because, if they were stopped by a police officer, he (father) would shoot the officer with the shotgun he kept between the car seats. Ellen described feeling terrified and driving as slowly and carefully as possible.

Prior to and when she was fifteen years old, Ellen reported that her father would pull down her pants and underpants to spank her bottom with his hand. Other family members recall this, as well. Once, the mother asked if he had "touched her" and Ellen felt unable to answer, not understanding what that meant. But she remembers that her father seemed to enjoy touching her bottom and would sometimes slip his hand between her legs.

Her mother recounted a family history of alcohol and drug abuse: On her husband's side of the family, his brother and nephew were both treated for alcoholism, with the nephew having committed suicide; her husband and his father were alcoholics, according to mental health professionals. Her mother described her own heavy drinking. Ellen and her younger brother have both been treated for alcoholism and drug addiction. Ellen's father gave her alcohol and drugs starting at age nine when he had parties with the neighbors and pornographic movies were watched. The children were invited to stay in the room during the movies and given alcohol and drugs. One of the neighbors started molesting Ellen when she was twelve years old and continued until she was fourteen and he moved out of the state.

At fifteen years old, Ellen was involved in a car accident when her father was driving while intoxicated. He hit a stone cliff while rounding a curve on a mountain road and the children were thrown from the car. Her father had picked up Tony and was threatening to throw him off the mountain when the police arrived and arrested him. After he was released from jail, he continued beating Ellen's mother and threatening her with a pistol he kept under his pillow.

Ellen left home when she was sixteen years old and found a job as a caretaker for an older woman whose daughter was a lawyer. Ellen, who lived in their garage apartment, became part of the family, studied for and took her GED (high school equivalency course), and enrolled at a community college. She attended Alcoholics Anonymous and stopped drinking. Taking a special interest in cooking, Ellen took cooking classes at the community college and began selling her own cooked products during lunch hour at the college. Demand grew and Ellen, after obtaining the proper permits, packaged her sandwiches, pies, and homemade chips, selling them in the larger community. She cooked after school classes were over and her elderly patient had gone to sleep. Ellen's patient and her daughter both enjoyed eating Ellen's food, themselves, and were glad for Ellen to cook in their kitchen.

After two years of developing her business, Ellen was nineteen years old and met Billy at the community college. She graduated while Billy dropped out, asking Ellen for dates and beginning to intrude in her life.

The Importance of History

It should be noted that the use of terms like *alcoholism* and *drug addiction* would be determined by the evaluator. For Loring, these terms are used when there has been a previous diagnosis and/or treatment for them; other terms like *alcohol use* or *drug use*, for example, could be useful when there is plenty of observation about this type of behavior.

Ellen's history helps lay the foundation for understanding her vulnerability when Billy became abusive toward her—emotionally, sexually, and physically. He punched and shoved her, called her "dumb" and "ugly," and made her watch violent pornography and participate in hurtful sexual activities, forcing objects into her (like soda bottles), unwilling to stop when she cried in pain.

Fortunately, the woman injured in Billy's car accident recovered. Some may wonder why Ellen was arrested when Billy had been drinking and driving. This is often the case with the coerced. With no regard for the coerced's safety or well-being, the coercer can involve them in dangerous and illegal activities. Often the coerced are captured as well, arrested and charged along with the coercer. While a police officer in Ellen's case suspected abuse, this is not always the case. In fact, the police officer separated Ellen from Billy and arranged for another officer to ride back to police headquarters with him. The police officer took Ellen in his car and discovered during the drive that Ellen was terrified of Billy's threat to kill her dog. The officer drove by Ellen's garage apartment, retrieved the dog, and dropped her pet off at the law office of the daughter of Ellen's patient. He then took Ellen on to police headquarters where she described the situation, now feeling confident about the safety of her dog.

Agreeing to testify against Billy, Ellen was freed on bond. When Billy was released from jail, also on bond, Ellen refused to see him and called the police twice when he showed up unannounced at her garage apartment.

When Cooperation Is Lacking

Unlike Ellen, some coerced women, when arrested, seem unwilling to talk with the police. They may appear angry and suspicious, speaking with disrespect to police officers or trying to hide their part in a crime. These women, when experiencing panic and fear from current and past experiences, can become agitated or even seem belligerent. They may not explain their fear or panic, having learned to cover it up with tough talk and angry language. This behavior may have been a survival technique when growing up in rough and dangerous families and neighborhoods.

Shocked by a crime that they were forced into, some of the coerced try to hide the crime or deny their participation. During evaluation, some of them have told me that they were trying to hide their participation from themselves, as well—so alien to their values and compassion was the crime. This postincident bizarre behavior can range from the coerced denying her presence at a crime to hiding evidence in strange places.

Psychosocial Evaluation: History of Relationships

A series of previous abusive relationships may be described in the same section as the relationship with the codefendant (the coercer): That would be called a "history of relationships." It can show a pattern in which the woman has experienced abuse and even coercion in multiple adult relationships.

Types of coercion and abuse would be included when describing her relationship with the coercer and in previous relationships. Documentation may include others who have witnessed interactions between the coerced and her partner, an interview with the coercer, previous and current police reports, and witness statements describing both of their roles in the crime. Previous family violence police reports can be helpful. If the coerced minimizes the abuse, others may have witnessed and understood her fear generated by his threats.

Psychosocial Evaluation
Jan Larson
History of Relationships

Jan described her first boyfriend, Jay, as hitting her, both slapping and punching. She remembered his throwing a clothes hamper, scissors, and knives at her. Three neighbors witnessed Jay's rage and this throwing behavior.

Her second boyfriend was not physically abusive, but would call her "whore," "worthless," and "good for nothing." He threatened that he would find her if she left him and pour acid on her face. Since he worked with chemicals at his job, Jan believed him. A workman interviewed by this evaluator heard this threat when the boyfriend was not aware of his presence in their home.

In her relationship with Kevin, her boyfriend at the time of the incident, Jan reported loving and fearing him at the same time. When this evaluator interviewed Kevin, he described their first year together as happy. He discussed the numerous restraining orders that had been imposed on him in previous relationships when he was physically abusive, but Kevin insisted that he had not physically harmed Jan. Kevin acknowledged that he always wanted to be in control during their relationship. Growing up, he was disciplined by his father who Kevin said would probably be in jail today for child abuse, since he kicked and beat him. Kevin told this evaluator that he did not hit Jan but he yelled at her, threatened her, and told Jan he'd kill their son if she left him.

Kevin was in the United States Army in Iraq and witnessed a friend shot and killed. He reported that he has been diagnosed with posttraumatic stress disorder at the veteran's hospital. Kevin said he started using crack. He then found that selling it was profitable. Kevin reported that he is "hot-headed" and said that he has checked up on Jan at the hospital where she works. He was suspicious that she was having sex with a doctor, but never found any evidence of it. Kevin said he followed her around because he wanted to see if she was really working or not. He explained about losing millions at the casinos where he goes to seek "action" which helps him relax. Toward the end of the interview, Kevin acknowledged that Jan might have, "gotten pushed or shoved by me unintentionally." He reported being proud of his service in the army and his current job as a city fire-fighter.

Kevin told this evaluator that Jan did not know about his selling crack until recently when she saw him selling on the front porch. She tried to talk him out of selling drugs, but he told her that he would burn down the house if she ever called the police. Kevin agreed with Jan's perceptions that he had isolated her from family and friends, listened to her telephone conversations, ordered her to perform sexual acts that made her uncomfortable, and drove her to and from the hospital where she worked.

Family and friends who were interviewed by this evaluator reported the isolation of Jan, who kept losing weight and appeared more and more depressed. It was difficult for them to intervene because Kevin seemed to be with her every minute when they were not working. He was observed ordering her to spend some of her salary on alcohol for him and his friends (she didn't drink alcohol). Her family members reported that she was always exhausted because, as she and Kevin told them, he would keep her up during the night to follow such orders as reading to him and washing his friends' clothes.

Jan remembered Kevin becoming more jealous and possessive after they married. They had previously dated for several months. She reported that Kevin rarely touched her in anger, but had shoved her against walls and counters several times. A witness reported hearing Kevin threaten to burn down the house. Jan had begged her not to call the police and they were not contacted. Jan described his tapping her on the head when she tried to sleep, keeping her awake to talk and read to him, so that she sometimes got very little sleep.

Kevin took a loan out on the house for home improvements. No improvements were made. According to a gambler interviewed by this evaluator, Kevin used the loan money to gamble. A neighbor, who is a frequent drug user, told this evaluator and the police that Kevin bragged about using the house loan money to buy cocaine.

A secretary at the house mortgage company reported that checks on Jan's bank account were used to pay the mortgage each month. Jan often wrote a note wishing the secretary well with her sick child, and Jan sometimes called the secretary to inquire about the child's health. A few weeks before the arrest of Jan and Kevin, Jan had called to inquire about the secretary's child and the secretary heard Kevin screaming at Jan in the background. She heard Kevin threaten to burn down the house unless Jan hung up the telephone immediately.

Jan reported to this evaluator that Kevin's threats increased just before their arrest, when he was using more crack with greater frequency. She had more difficulty concentrating in her job as an emergency room nurse. Jan described her own obedience to him when he threatened to harm their daughter or burn down the house. Jan tried to delay his follow through on any of the threats by seeming to obey Kevin's orders. She described being frightened by Kevin's recent orders that she must answer the door and take money handed to her, while handing the person an envelope. Once she refused to do this and Kevin grabbed their daughter and threatened to choke her until Jan promised to obey. He then handed her the child.

The Purpose of the History of Relationships Section

The documentation of relational interaction through collateral witness reports and documents obtained/reviewed is useful in painting a picture of the coerced's relationship history. She may not be aware of the total picture, having shut out or minimized some of her terror in order to survive. In each of her relationships, Jan was described as staring into space and sometimes seeming to be unaware (dissociating), withdrawn, and not having very good concentration or memory.

In some cases, an investigator can help identify important collateral witnesses. When an investigator is not available, the evaluator may ask the client and other collateral witnesses for suggestions for others to interview, as well as ideas about important documents to review.

In Jan's work as a nurse, she had a rule for herself: When taking care of patients, she must be able to focus on the task or excuse herself when recalling frightening orders from Kevin. She would get other coverage if dissociation started. Evaluating coercion should include the impact of coercion on the coerced's other relationships, work, driving, and self-care.

Jan's daughter (seven years old) was able to describe threats and Jan's efforts to keep her safe. The police, attorneys, and judge understood her dilemma and a plea bargain resulted in Jan being able to keep her job as a nurse. She decided to seek therapy and attends weekly support group meetings at a nearby battered women's shelter. Jan described feeling like she had escaped captivity in what should have been a loving relationship, and she never wants to be in a "living prison" again.

Trauma Chart

A trauma chart can be a valuable part of a psychosocial evaluation. This chart helps others to understand both the history of relationships and the amount/type of trauma the coerced has experienced. Information for this chart can come from interviewing the coerced and collateral witnesses, as well as reviewing documents. Additionally, police, hospital, education, therapy, and doctors' reports may also provide information.

A trauma chart is a history, a timeline. If trauma is present, a chart helps others understand and visualize it. Actually, many of the coerced have expressed that seeing a trauma chart helped them get a clearer understanding of their own lives.

Betsy's Life of Continuous Abuse

Betsy drove the getaway car for her husband's bank robbery. She explained to the police and later to me that she did not know he was going to commit a robbery. Focused on her fear of his hurting both her son and dog, she simply obeyed his orders, one by one, without considering what they all added up to. So when her husband, Nick, delivered a string of orders, she complied: Put the poodle in her crate (though the dog usually stayed in the house each day); call the day care to tell them their son had a doctor's appointment (he did not); drive the car to the day care to pick up Jeff; put Jeff in the back seat while Kevin sat in the passenger seat; drop Jeff off at her mother's house; pull up on the side of the bank and wait for him after he threatened to kill Jeff and her mother if she was not waiting for him when he came out of the bank and if she did not drive away quickly; drive back to their house when he exited the bank. Betsy had gaps in her memory of the bank robbery and her role in driving the get-away car.

> I know I should remember what happened. But it was like a horror movie. And I only remember pieces, like when we picked up Jeff and dropped him off at Mom's. But I don't remember leaving Mom's house. I really believed him. I had to do what he said or he'd hurt Jeff and Mom. But I don't remember much about waiting at the bank. I was gripping the wheel tight. I could hardly breathe. I panicked and had to get out of the car for a few minutes. I felt closed in and trapped. He ran out and jumped in the car carrying a satchel with a gun poking out. I stopped breathing. I remember him yelling. But I don't know what he said. I remember bumping into a curb when I made a turn. We stayed in the house for two days. He wouldn't let me answer the phone. All the curtains were drawn. Nick was doing cocaine and peeking out windows. He let me answer the phone once. I lied and said it was Mom. A pizza man came and I knew he was police. They had told me on the phone to let him in but not tell Nick. I let him in and he tackled Nick.

Betsy Wiley
Trauma Timeline

3–6 years old	Repeatedly burned by mother
	Cried a lot
	Seemed depressed
	Often no food in house
7–10 years old	Sexually molested by uncle
	Saw father abusing mother
11–13 years old	Beaten and bullied in school
	Bullied by her brothers
14 years old	Raped by a neighbor
15–20 years old	Two abusive boyfriends
	Self-medicated/drug addiction
	Therapy for addiction
21–25 years old	Graduated nursing school
	No further drug use
26 years old	Married Nick: abuse/coercion
27 years old	Son born
28 years old	The incident

Betsy's Capture and Plea Bargain

Relief after arrest is common among the coerced. Even jail is a welcomed freedom where no one is threatening or harming her. Many women reveal that being in jail is the first experience in a long time where they are not frightened, and they even feel appreciated. Betsy felt free and safe away from Nick. She read poetry to the other women in jail. That said, the coercer's attempts to threaten and control often do not stop after capture. Betsy received notes from Nick, which were against jail rules. She informed the major whenever it happened and turned over the notes to her lawyer. These notes contained instructions to not discuss the bank robbery.

After her arrest, Betsy was open and cooperative with detectives. Police interviewed witnesses who saw her get out of the car at the bank, appearing frightened and struggling to breathe. One even asked if she was alright, giving Betsy a hug during which Betsy told her she was scared but couldn't say why for fear of the bystander being harmed. Within a few minutes, this same bystander, who was outside smoking, saw Nick run back to the car, take Betsy by the hair and sling her into the driver's seat, and hold a gun to her head while she drove the car away. Police believed the bystander's account of the incident, although Betsy didn't remember the gun held against her head until she was told about the witness's statement. Betsy received sympathy and understanding from police and the court, where her willingness to testify against Nick resulted in a plea bargain that involved a short period of probation without serving time in jail.

A trauma history timeline helped the lawyers and the court during Betsy's plea bargain. Usually the items listed on a chart are documented by collateral witnesses and/or documents. There are occasions when documentation and witnesses are difficult to locate. It is helpful for the evaluator to be well versed in research and literature about trauma and abuse in order to assess the situation accurately, and relevant research can be brought into the testimony when appropriate.

Psychosocial Evaluation: The Incident

A description of the incident is usually based on police reports, witness statements, and the coerced's report of her role and possible coercion. It is helpful to interview witnesses and, although often not possible, it can be productive to interview the coercer, himself. As suggested previously, his lawyer might not want him giving information that could be brought up in court. The problem in gaining access to interview the coercer exists whether they have separate trials or not. It can also be valuable for the evaluator to visit the incident scene and/or view crime scene photographs/drawings in order to better understand the coerced's descriptions of the incident. When videos of crime scenes are available, they can be helpful, as well. All of the documents/videos reviewed would be noted in the introduction of the psychosocial evaluation.

The Involvement of Ellen in Financial Fraud

Like many other coerced women, Ellen had tunnel vision where she did not see the final purpose of the many discrete orders she obeyed. Her husband, Ray, instructed her to collect money from family and friends to invest in a construction project. He demanded that she contribute a large portion of the money she had been given as gifts from her parents. When Ellen expressed concern about selling her investments and putting two hundred thousand dollars in one single project, Ray yelled that she didn't trust him; nor did she support his work as an investment counselor. Neighbors heard him shouting at her and witnessed him chase her beagle out of the house and around the yard. One of the neighbors rescued the dog and threatened to call police.

Ellen, a high school teacher, brought brochures of Ray's construction project to share with teachers and staff at her school (as he had instructed): The new condominiums appeared attractive and the brochure described significant financial gains for those investing at the beginning of construction. When Ray ordered Ellen to talk with her family about investments, she was hesitant, but he was heard by her brother saying that he would leave her if she couldn't trust and support him.

Her brother saw bruises on Ellen's neck and she admitted to him that Ray had choked her. But she explained that he had apologized and was nervous about getting enough investors. Ellen did approach family members about the project and several of them invested, along with friends and neighbors.

Within months, investors began demanding some of the promised money, but Ray explained that things were taking longer to build than expected. For those who drove to the condominium construction site in a nearby town, no building could be seen on the land. Some neighbors hired a lawyer and an investigation was begun by the police, who discovered that there was no planned construction. Ray was spending the money for a new boat and gambling trips. Both Ellen and Ray were arrested for theft.

Ellen had followed each of Ray's orders: She sought out investors, obtained estimates for various parts of the construction, and applied for city and county permits. The demands from Ray were handled by Ellen as separate entities. Much later, after they were both arrested, Ellen realized that Ray had never made a down payment for any service or building contract, just kept collecting investments.

Ellen's anguish stemmed from the disappointment and anger of neighbors and family members who had invested. Teachers and school staff had used savings to invest with the hope of earning additional funds for college and retirement funds. There was anger and resentment toward both Ellen and Ray, and many saw Ellen as knowing about the fraud, but soliciting their investments anyway. When they attended court proceedings and heard about Ray's coercion, physical and emotional abuse, and Ellen's medical treatment for injuries, some became convinced that she was coerced and unaware of his plot. Ellen was sure of his innocence for several weeks after their arrest. "I was so sure the police were wrong about him. He talked with me about plans for constructing the condominiums."

In this situation, threats to abandon were the primary form of emotional abuse. Ellen felt abandoned by her parents who divorced and pursued their own lives; neither spent much time with her. During their two-year marriage, he isolated Ellen from family and friends. Ray surveilled her and demanded total obedience. He controlled Ellen's behavior by threatening to leave their home and move out of the country. To convince Ellen that he'd actually abandon her, Ray had left once and did not return for a few days.

Psychosocial Evaluation
Ellen Dwyer
The Incident

During the three-month financial fraud (from January, 2013, to March, 2013) by her husband, Ray Dwyer, Ellen Dwyer sold investments in the alleged condominium project, obtained city and county permits for construction, and consulted with construction and other companies about prices for their services. At her husband's insistence, she invested two hundred thousand dollars of her own money, which was given as gifts by her mother and father.

During interviews with this evaluator, many of the collateral witnesses discussed their impression that Ellen seemed to believe in the project and had expressed both excitement and fear about investing so much of her own money. She told a number of investors that Ray had assured her that she'd receive a 20 percent gain from her investment within three to six months.

Those family members and neighbors spending time with Ray and Ellen were quick to acknowledge his ordering her around and his demands for loyalty and obedience. His anger at Ellen when she didn't obey quickly enough had been observed.

Psychosocial Evaluation: Diagnosis and Impact of Diagnosis on the Incident

These two components of the psychosocial evaluation aim at assessing abuse, coercion, and trauma, if they exist, as well as whether and how coercion influenced the person at the time of an incident. They can appear as separate sections or be combined.

Diagnosis in the mental health field is often based on a multiaxis approach (American Psychiatric Association, 2013). Each axis covers an important area of functioning in the attempt to give a picture of someone that includes such important aspects as the primary diagnosis, personality issues, stresses, and medical problems.

When coercion, abuse, and trauma are discovered, it is helpful for the diagnosis to include the sources of trauma and coercion, as well as their impact. Trauma may have been diagnosed in the past (during previous therapy, medical treatment, or evaluations), and this can also be included. When trauma is present, it is valuable to describe symptoms and indicate whether/how they impacted the coerced's behavior (especially at the time of the incident). As suggested earlier, diagnosis as a term used in psychosocial evaluations included in this book means all of these dimensions. Individual evaluators may emphasize one or more of these dimensions.

The Diagnosis of Rose

Rose had a history of mental health problems and abusive relationships. In the incident, she stabbed her husband, Andy. He was an army veteran who had not recovered from his trauma in Afghanistan. Having grown up with grandparents who were concentration camp survivors from Germany, he seemed constantly fearful and anxious, telling Rose that no one was safe in any country. He terrified Rose with threats to kill her while aiming guns at her head and at her daughters, Andy's stepdaughters. He would shout for Rose to kill him, sometimes handing her a knife. In treatment at the veteran's hospital, Andy had been diagnosed with PTSD. Having called the police on several occasions, Rose was considering leaving and divorcing Andy when the incident occurred. Andy slapped a butcher knife in Rose's hands and shouted for her to stab him or he would shoot both of her daughters.

He had seemed more agitated and rageful that day and Rose saw his finger on the trigger when Andy aimed the gun at Sarah and Lisa, her daughters. She did not remember afterward, but Rose stabbed Andy once in the chest, grabbed Sarah and Lisa, and ran out of the house. A neighbor called the police and took the girls while Rose ran back into the house, following the 911 operator's instructions to help Andy. He died on the way to the hospital.

For Rose's evaluation, previous hospital and mental health treatment records were obtained. Mental health records from the jail were also helpful.

Psychosocial Evaluation
Rose Hepson
Diagnosis

Rose has a history of depression and anxiety. She has been treated at Center Regional Hospital (1996, 1998, 2000); at Osforth Hospital (2004, 2007, 2010); at

Hill County Mental Health (2012); and at Tobin Mental Health Center (2012). She was diagnosed with a major depression, as well as anxiety with panic attacks. Rose has taken Zoloft, Xanax, and Elavil. At the Hill County Jail, Rose was diagnosed with posttraumatic stress disorder (PTSD) and given Risperdal and Zoloft. Her mental health treatment records at the jail contain information about visual hallucinations: She sees the victim, Andy, each night and apologizes to him. She is also described as having panic attacks at the jail when she remembers his threats to kill her if she left him.

Rose has completed her high school equivalency studies and passed her GED test at Hill County Jail. She has difficulty concentrating and sitting still due to her trauma and anxiety. But the teacher allows her additional time to study and take tests; she was allowed to take the tests in a quiet room by herself because she jumps and panics when hearing loud noises. Called hypervigilance as a trauma symptom, any loud noise disrupts Rose's concentration and focus: This causes Rose to cry, shake, and withdraw from others. According to her teacher in the jail, Rose often looks around the room to feel safer. The minister who gives Bible study daily gave Rose a Bible and a study guide, which he reads each day for an hour with Rose. She has obtained a scholarship from a local college for two correspondence courses. She received an A in one course and is working on another.

Rose receives counseling weekly from a social worker at the jail. The social worker wrote in reports that, with medication and counseling, Rose's trauma has improved and she rarely has panic attacks, but there are periods of time when Rose dissociates—staring off into space and not remembering what she had been doing. The social worker noted in the chart that this dissociation is one of her symptoms of posttraumatic stress disorder, along with high anxiety and fearfulness.

Rose continues to experience PTSD with some anxiety and depression. She occasionally has auditory and visual hallucinations, seeing and hearing the victim, who is deceased. She is horrified by having harmed him, although she also feared for the lives of herself and her daughters, whom he was threatening to kill, according to interviews with Rose and her daughters.

Impact of Diagnosis on the Incident

Rose had posttraumatic stress disorder during and after the incident. During the incident, she experienced panic, believing that he would shoot her daughters like his having shot their dog in her presence a few weeks previously. She has had a history of abusive relationships and, prior to her relationship with Andy, was hospitalized twice for injuries from family violence.

At the time of the incident, Rose feared for her own life and the lives of her daughters. Overwhelmed with anxiety, Rose disassociated during the incident and does not remember having stabbed Andy one time in the chest. However, seeing the knife in her hand and the blood on Andy's chest, she deduced that she had done this and, after seeking safety for her daughters, immediately called 911 and carried out instructions to apply pressure to his chest. She was giving him mouth-to-mouth resuscitation when the police arrived.

Rose's Sentence

Rose was sentenced to a prison term. While serving time in prison, she completed several classes, including courses in trauma and battered women's issues. An aunt took care of her daughters, who visited their mother as well as talking with her on the telephone.

PSYCHOSOCIAL EVALUATION:
THE RECOMMENDATION SECTION

The recommendation section involves the evaluator considering possible options: What kind of intervention would help to repair damage done to victims? And which interventions would satisfy the need for the community to be protected? What would be helpful for possible depression, trauma, and coercion in the coerced person's history and possibly current life?

In a recent case, Loring testified about the coercion experienced by a woman who was accused of failing to protect her child from her boyfriend's neglect. When he withheld food, she would sneak the child food to prevent confrontations where he would threaten to harm the child. The attorneys wanted a plea bargain but could not agree on a sentence. Her behavior was not in question. The issue involved her choosing the lesser of what she saw as two evils: Her daughter being beaten or having food withheld. She managed to slip the child food by pretending to bring her water and crackers (all that was allowed) and hiding fruit and sandwiches under her sweater.

The judge (there was no jury) asked questions during the expert testimony. He then sentenced the woman to a period of time in prison. He followed Loring's recommendations for the woman upon her release from prison: She would be on parole, which included living in a residential treatment program for alcohol addiction, as well as receiving therapy for trauma and abuse. This woman had a history of using alcohol to self-medicate when anxious and depressed. The residential treatment program had counseling and addiction groups. Loring also recommended psychotherapy at a nearby agency where there was a sliding fee scale that the woman could afford when she reentered the work force as a waitress (her previous occupation, which she loved). Loring also suggested that weekly meetings at the battered woman shelter would help with her history of abusive relationships and experience with coercion.

SPECIAL CONSIDERATIONS

High-Profile Cases

In the case mentioned above, there was a great deal of publicity, including television coverage. After the court hearing, when there was testimony and the plea bargain was accepted, greater understanding developed about conditions that the coerced woman had experienced.

For high profile cases in which feelings are strong among some in the community (and throughout the country), evaluators who testify should be alert and careful about their own safety. For example, after testimony, asking a courthouse deputy for an escort to the car is very appropriate.

Ethical issues are also relevant in high-profile cases. Reporters may ask for interviews with experts. However, with the possibility of future appeals or bringing to light personal information that could have remained private (not used in court testimony), an expert needs to be cautious to avoid sharing information hurtful to the client.

Complex Issues among Some of the Coerced

The coerced may present themselves with more than the issue of coercion. While depression can be reactive to their current abuse, some have experienced abuse throughout their lives and severe depression could have begun in childhood. The coerced sometimes use drugs and/or alcohol to medicate themselves. And other disorders need to be considered, just as a thorough exploration of possible diagnoses would be part of evaluating any client or patient.

Careful observation needs to be directed to any physical problems experienced by the coerced, many of whom have been slammed against walls, hit on the head with hard objects, and brutalized in other ways. Complaints of headaches, stomachaches, and other physical pain should be evaluated by a physician or specialist. Difficulties with memory, problem solving, or cognitive processes can be evaluated by a psychologist and/or a neurologist. A psychological test is valuable when neurological functioning seems impaired or the IQ is important to know. Anxiety that is unmanageable can point to the need for a psychiatric examination and possible medication. Complex issues presented by the coerced need to be assessed and considered, with the appropriate specialist included.

There is sometimes a dilemma regarding when psychotherapy for the traumatized coerced can take place. The honest condition of a coerced person needs to be presented during court proceedings. After what is often a long time of anguish and not being heard, the coerced must describe their experiences truthfully with genuine feelings. What is the coerced and traumatized woman to do with the profound symptoms of complex trauma prior to the trial? How would she handle anxiety without therapy prior to the completion of court proceedings, which can sometimes take a long time? Medication can be prescribed by a psychiatrist and certainly support is important. But the issue is whether or not to disrupt the coercive and traumatic issues that need to be conveyed during court proceedings—whether healing can be started sooner rather than later.

Evaluating Pet/Animal Abuse

All psychosocial evaluations should include exploration of possible pet/ animal abuse. For the evaluator, pet abuse is sickening to hear about or witness through verbal accounts or pictures. Of course, the coerced and their children witnessing pet abuse are traumatized as well. There are many cases where horror is visited upon animals in order to harm or direct behaviors of the coerced. In research with the coerced about the nature of threats, pet abuse was identified as a means of coercing women into illegal behavior (Loring and Beaudoin, 2000).

A valuable tool for understanding animal abuse is *Animal Abuse and Family Violence: Linkages, Research and Implications for Professional Practice* (Loring, Geffner, and Marsh, 2007). The book is a collection of interesting articles that examine such problems as the fear among abused women when leaving home if the pet is not allowed in the shelter and so is left with the abuser. Efforts to create safe places for animals are needed to encourage the flight of abused women to safety. Grief and guilt among the coerced is huge when they believe they have failed to protect their beloved animals from harm or death. In their minds, they revisit the scene over and over, helpless to figure out what they could have done differently to have saved their loved one from pain and/or death. And those evaluators, therapists, and other helpers who hear about these atrocities must find ways to deal with their own feelings.

Genograms

Genograms can be a helpful tool in describing the total context of coercion. The genogram is a diagram of family relationships (and significant others) (see figure 8.1 that follows). Circles represent women and squares are used for men. Various shaped lines (sometimes colored) travel from one person (or animal) to another, symbolizing the type of relationship between them. In the genogram that follows a railroad track–like line would represent an emotionally abusive relationship, as can be seen in the key, and a triple line would indicate coercion. Some genogram programs have suggestions for which line means a specific type of relationship, but experts often select their own meanings and create a key that shows which lines indicate what kind of treatment, as in the genogram that follows.

For a coerced woman, the circles and squares with a name on each could include her parents, siblings, or anyone important in her life. A genogram can have pets and other significant others, such as a teacher, counselor, or influential neighbor. Thus, a genogram is like a map of how the coerced person came to be the person she is, including abusive and harmful relationships, past and current. When testifying, a genogram can be used in the form of a large chart. A valuable tool for learning more about and creating genograms is *Genograms: Assessment and Intervention* by McGoldrick, Gerson, and Shellenberger (1999).

In the example that follows, Annie's genogram, there are more explanatory terms than would normally be found in a genogram, such as "grandfather" and "the coerced." This was done to help clarify identities. Each person's name is below his/her circle or square. While this clarity is especially important here, one may also use relationship identifications (brother, father) for genograms used in court. Other times one can explain the relationships verbally during expert testimony while pointing to the genogram. If it is a chart, the size should be large enough for the jury/judge to see.

"Annie—The Coerced" is represented by a circle half filled with black, indicating an alcohol problem which had previously been diagnosed as alcoholism. When the upper-right-hand corner of a square or circle is filled with black, this indicates drug addiction in this genogram. The evaluator needs to be clear on the definitions of alcoholism and drug addiction and it is helpful when previous diagnoses confirm this, although evidence can be gathered for documentation. Since many others in her family have also been diagnosed as having drug addiction and/or alcoholism, their circles and squares are also half black and/or with black in the square/circle upper-right quarter. Alcoholism and drug addiction can often be present in multiple family members, suggesting genetic and modeling issues where these behaviors may be learned, along with possible predispositions. A jagged line represents physical abuse. Where there are arrows connected to lines, the arrows point to the victim. In Annie's genogram, her father (Sam) physically abused her mother (Betsy). And Sam has been diagnosed as having both alcoholism and drug addiction, as indicated by the bottom half and the top-right corner of his square both being filled with black.

Looking at the genogram, one can see that Annie was physically and emotionally abused, as well as coerced by her husband, Peter. Annie's dog, Charly, was killed by Peter, thus the X in this box, indicating death. And their teenage child, Suzi, was emotionally abused by Peter, as well as coerced (threatened with physical abuse unless she obeyed such orders as obtaining illegal drugs for her father). Annie's grandmother Louise neglected her mother, Betsy, as indicated by the line with two circles. And Annie's grandfather Gerald physically abused his son (her father, Sam) as shown by the jagged line.

When coercion is present, it is important for the genogram to demonstrate all who are coerced and harmed. This includes other family members, animals, pets, neighbors, friends, work colleagues, and others. A genogram about coercion should be inclusive so that all patterns and types of coercive experiences are portrayed, like the death of Annie's dog at the hands of her husband, Peter, who used the dog, Charly, to threaten and force obedience from Annie. How this coercion occurred can be covered during explanations of a genogram and/or in a report describing the genogram.

Other important factors can be included in a genogram and/or in a description of the history. Some of these factors include children exposed to pesticides or lead, special education that may indicate learning difficulties, poverty, childhood hunger and neglect such as failure to seek medical care, dangerous neighborhoods, childhood head injuries, prejudice and racism, absence of a parent, or other significant experiences. These conditions can impact a person's life in ways that may create vulnerabilities to coercion and difficulties in escaping coercion, such as low self-esteem due, in part, to learning difficulties and poor school performance.

ANNIE'S GENOGRAM

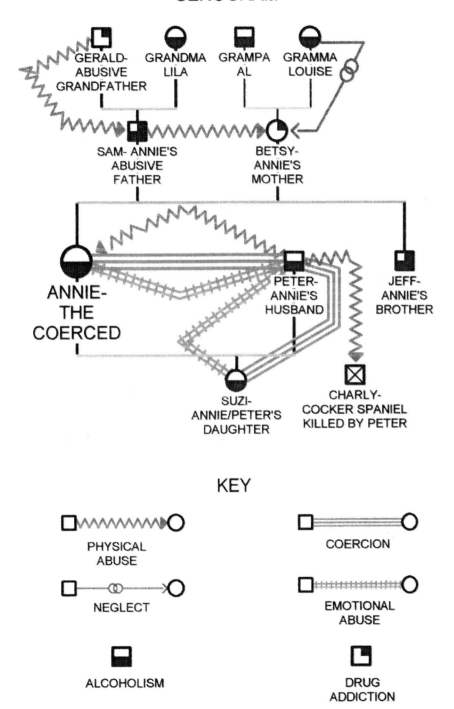

GERALD- ABUSIVE GRANDFATHER

GRANDMA LILA

GRAMPA AL

GRAMMA LOUISE

SAM- ANNIE'S ABUSIVE FATHER

BETSY- ANNIE'S MOTHER

ANNIE- THE COERCED

PETER- ANNIE'S HUSBAND

JEFF- ANNIE'S BROTHER

SUZI- ANNIE/PETER'S DAUGHTER

CHARLY- COCKER SPANIEL KILLED BY PETER

KEY

PHYSICAL ABUSE

COERCION

NEGLECT

EMOTIONAL ABUSE

ALCOHOLISM

DRUG ADDICTION

Figure 8.1.

9

Coercion in Other Groups

Immigrants, People with Disabilities, LGBT, Church Partners, Children, Adolescents, and Elders

Judith Herman (1997) noted that the terror of traumatic events creates a need for protective attachments yet traumatized people may alternate between isolation and clinging, having lost trust in themselves, others, and God. Human struggles cross cultural lines: Sadly, abuse knows no bounds.

COERCION AMONG IMMIGRANTS

For immigrants coming to the United States, the presence and pain of abuse and coercion are influenced by aspects of their cultures. Focusing on Chinese and South Asian immigrant women, Midlarsky, Venkata-ramani-Kothari, and Plante (2006) explored types of abuse and cultural factors. Although they described abuse in the South Asian community as similar to abuse among Americans, there were some differences. One kind of physical abuse in the South Asian community involved throwing hot oil on the victim (whereas Loring has had only one such case during thirty years of doing evaluations among Americans). The researchers observed that South Asian men usually control finances whether or not a woman works.

> If an employed woman is married to a dominating man, she may not have the opportunity to enjoy the independence and identity that she has earned. For example, among South Asians, men usually control the family finances regardless of the woman's working status. (p. 289)

These women learn from childhood that they would inflict the greatest harm on their family if they were bad wives and their marriages ended (Ayyub, 2000). For some women, this could mean accepting domination rather than leaving an abusive situation.

When battered women from any country are immigrants living in the United States, their citizenship status is often a source of threats from their coercive partner. Living with their children in the United States, these women feel an urgent need to obey the coercer's orders in order to avoid his threats of causing her deportation and separation from their children whom he would keep in America. It is usually not clear to the coerced whether these threats are realistic or even possible. But many believe this could happen and fear losing their children if they are returned to their country.

It is important that an evaluator discover abuse when it is present among immigrants. If language is a problem, translators can assist with this effort. In some immigrant abuse cases, laws allow that violence may be a mitigating factor that can help a woman stay in America with her children. Evidence and explanations about a woman experiencing abuse and coercion may serve as mitigation to prevent deportation.

Wen

The evaluation of Wen from South Asia took place in her lawyer's office to protect Wen from her husband, who kept a close watch on her. Wen's husband had ordered her to cover up his drug sales. Wen reported different threats, such as having her deported so that she would never see her daughter again; or he would sell their daughter into sex trafficking.

Although her husband, Chai, was unwilling to talk with Loring, a number of witnesses were interviewed on the condition that their identities remain secret: They feared Chai's possible revenge. They had overheard his threats toward Wen and witnessed him forcing her to remain silent about his having made their home a center for selling drugs. One witness saw Chai kill a man in front of Wen and others.

Wen received a plea offer in which she would be on probation after testifying in Chai's trial: She agreed to this. However, Chai accepted a plea and no testimony was needed. Wen and other witnesses expressed great relief. It can be stressful for everyone, including the expert witness, when there appears to be the possibility of danger associated with testifying. Wen decided to continue her education and enrolled in cooking classes at a local college. After completing her studies, she got a job in an elegant hotel and was successful in helping them create international dishes. Wen took her daughter and left Chai, who had been released from prison on bond. She felt relief at her freedom from threats and decided to pursue U.S. citizenship. She said, "I had always hoped to cook in a restaurant. Customers make special requests that I cook. And I come out of the kitchen to greet them. I love my job!"

Psychosocial Evaluation
Wen Rhis
Impact of Diagnosis on the Incident

Wen was terrified by her husband's threats, especially to sell their daughter into sex trafficking. She believed that he was capable of carrying out this threat. Her sister, Lili, and friend, Asche Wykoff, who witnessed this repeated threat, also described it as credible and frightening. Her husband also threatened to cause Wen's deportation, insisting that she would never see her daughter again. This was a part of the trauma that Wen experienced, as well as a sense of helplessness and fear associated with emotional, physical, and sexual abuse. Wen was repeatedly raped by her husband, who also allowed key drug buyers to rape her.

Wen suffered from Post-traumatic Stress Disorder, which included a number of symptoms: She was overwhelmed with anxiety and fear, continually looked around the room (hypervigilance), jumped at any noise (startle response), and had difficulty concentrating because of thoughts that intruded on her thinking (intrusive thoughts). Wen spent all of her time in the back of the house in her bedroom and her daughter's room, as well as cooking in the kitchen. Avoiding the front living and dining rooms, she had little contact with the drug sales that occurred there. She even used the back door to exit and enter the house. Wen avoided thinking about and interacting with the people involved with her husband's drug activities.

Wen was unaware of the conflict over drug sales until she heard shots from the front rooms. Her daughter recalled baking a birthday cake for her teacher when she and her mother (Wen) heard the shots. Wen immediately removed all hot items from the stove top and turned off the oven, fearful of her husband's past threats to throw hot cooking oil on her. The daughter remembered that Wen pulled her underneath the kitchen table where the table cloth made it into a tent. They called the police on Wen's cell phone and heard sirens approaching. Ms. Jetson, a next door neighbor, kept the child while Wen was taken to the police station and questioned.

Wen's trauma and fear prevented her from sharing information earlier about the drug activity in her home. She was terrified of threats by her husband who coerced her into silence. She felt hopeless about having a happy life and thought about killing herself, although Wen states she would not kill herself because she'd never abandon her child.

She expressed love for the United States and hopes to make a life here for herself and her daughter. She discussed deep regret about illegal activities that occurred in her home.

COERCION IN THE LGBT COMMUNITY

Duke and Davidson (2009) reviewed literature in the area of intimate part-ner violence (IPV) in their article, "Same-Sex Intimate Partner Violence: Lesbian, Gay, and Bisexual Affirmative Outreach and Advocacy." They pointed out that violence occurs across the lines of gender and sexual orientation. A specific problem arises for gays and bisexuals when they contemplate reaching out for help since there is a lack of sensitivity to gay issues. These authors argue that organizations need to increase sensitivity around gay issues and include the abusive experiences of same-sex part-ners in any advocacy training. The authors suggested that organizations should develop and advertise programs that provide services for those experiencing same-sex abuse (Duke and Davidson, 2009).

Coercion can involve threats to make sexual orientation public. This type of coercion may be used when someone has chosen to keep sexual orientation private for a variety of reasons.

Coercion of Mark by Joe

Joe and Mark were in an intimate relationship for five years when Joe's controlling behavior increased. Mark lost a job when his company moved out of state and he was having difficulty finding another job in his spe-cialty area—geography. Joe was critical and demeaning previously, but his abuse increased to the extent that friends and both of their families noticed and commented about Joe's put-downs and distain toward Mark.

Mark looked for therapy and felt comfortable at a gay counseling cen-ter where he saw a counselor weekly and a psychiatrist once a month; the psychiatrist prescribed medication for anxiety and depression. When Mark told his counselor about Joe's treatment, the counselor described Joe's remarks as more humorous than critical, suggesting that Mark work to improve his sense of humor and stop being so sensitive.

Mark found a job as a salesman at a clothing store. He worked hard and was soon promoted to department manager, while also selling clothes on occasion. His sense of style and interpersonal skills made him popular and customers waited for his help, even when other salespeople were available.

Managing a sports equipment store, Joe seemed jealous and angry, since Mark's salary was larger than his and Mark's circle of friends was growing. Previously, Joe had isolated Mark from others, and the two had only a few close friends. Now, when Joe worked late, Mark had dinner with his new friends. Mark thought he saw Joe watching him from a dis-tance during dinner with friends one evening but, when he asked about it, Joe denied his surveillance.

Joe began coming into the store where Mark worked. Mark observed him stealing an expensive tie. At Mark's exclusive store, all staff members were required to sign an honor code, promising not to steal merchandise and to report any theft they witnessed or heard about.

Joe's shoplifting behavior occurred every few weeks, always involving an expensive piece of merchandise—and always where Mark could see the theft, although others did not witness it. Mark talked to Joe about his behavior, but Joe only denied any theft.

Mark loved his dog, but Joe had never been fond of animals, even appearing jealous of Mark's affection toward his poodle, Frankie. When Mark noticed that Frankie was limping, he took the poodle for medical treatment. The doctor found that Frankie's leg was broken and put on a cast. Mark asked Joe what might have happened, and Joe said the poodle had gotten in his (Joe's) way on the stairs and Joe had kicked him down the stairs. And, Joe had added, that was nothing compared to what would happen if Mark reported "any imagined thefts," as Joe called them. Further, Joe promised that, if Mark left him, Frankie would be found dead in a yard, probably mauled by some stray dog.

Mark felt terrified, adjusting his work hours so that Joe wouldn't be alone with Frankie. Feeling coerced into silence, Mark considered leaving his job. The store owner, who had been supportive and encouraging, brought Mark into his office and asked what was wrong, since Mark seemed depressed. But Mark was afraid to tell him.

A store detective saw Joe take a scarf and put it in his pocket when Mark was across the room with a clear view of the theft. He took Joe to a back room and called police, who also questioned Mark. Mark told the detective and owner about the thefts, threats, and injury to his dog. Both of them were arrested. When Mark was released on bond, he quickly moved out of the house, but his fear continued when he saw Joe surveilling him across the street from his new apartment. Mark felt depressed and hopeless. "I was caught in an impossible situation and chose the safest path for my dog. Joe even seemed nice to me when I kept my silence, and pretty nice to my poodle, too. I betrayed Troy's trust. He owns the store and helped me a lot."

When Mark's lawyer asked for an evaluation for his client, Loring's collateral witness "wish list" included Joe, as well as family, neighbors, and friends who had witnessed emotional abuse and coercion. Interviews with the animal hospital staff revealed that Joe, in a previous relationship several years ago, had injured another dog as a means of controlling the owner, his former partner. Staff at the hospital reported that Mark seemed very upset when his poodle was injured. Mark gave them a letter asking that Joe never be allowed to pick up Mark's dog from the hospital.

Psychosocial Evaluation
Mark Allen Thompson
Impact of Diagnosis on the Incident of Theft

At the Healey Counseling Center, Dr. Fred Maz diagnosed Mark Thompson as suffering from the posttraumatic stress disorder in February, 2013. During psychotherapy and medicine visits in February and March, Mr. Thompson told Dr. Maz and his counselor about abuse and coercion by his partner, Joe Tyler. Dr. Maz reported that Mr. Thompson had the following trauma symptoms: Anxiety, frequent nightmares, poor appetite, difficulty concentrating, and flashbacks. Saying he felt better when he didn't discuss his feelings, Mr. Thompson stopped therapy and medicine visits in late March. Dr. Maz suggested in his notes that Mr. Thompson was "using avoidance, characteristic of the Posttraumatic stress disorder."

Family and friends noticed that Mr. Thompson was experiencing increasing depression and isolation during January, February, and March, 2013. His parents reported that Mr. Thompson seemed anxious and upset when his dog was found to have a broken leg. After that, if he had to stay late at work, Mr. Thompson would leave his poodle, Frankie, with this parents.

Four staff members at the Stevens Animal Hospital were interviewed by this evaluator (Dr. Matt and Dr. Stevens, technician Lewis Anderson, and receptionist Lynn Harper). After the discovery of his dog's broken leg, Mr. Thompson was described as anxious, stuttering, and crying. Dr. Stevens discussed Mr. Thompson with this evaluator: "He seemed traumatized and in real anguish. He said his boyfriend had hurt the dog. I remembered several years ago when this guy had hurt another dog. So I called the police this time and reported him. Then, about a week later, we heard about them both being arrested. After he was released from jail, Mark visited with me and told me about the thefts and said he was afraid to report his boyfriend. I think he was afraid his dog would be killed."

Mr. Thompson was experiencing continued traumatic experiences while being coerced by his partner, who refused to be interviewed by this evaluator. Mr. Thompson witnessed his partner's thefts but feared reporting them would result in additional harm to his dog. Coerced into silence, an additional component of his trauma involved going against his own values. He liked his job and felt remorseful about disappointing the store owner.

Traumatized and concerned about the safety of his poodle, Mr. Thompson avoided dealing with, or reporting, the thefts by his partner. Hoping for an end to his coercive experience, Mr. Thompson waited for it to be over, feeling helpless, fearful and anxious. He watched for signs of danger, and experienced repeated emotional abuse when called "stupid" and "worthless." Exhausted and depressed, Mr. Thompson had symptoms of complex posttraumatic stress disorder that interfered with his problem-solving skills: He was exhausted from vigilance while watching for dangerous cues and harmful behavior toward him and his pet.

An Understanding Victim

The store manager had a daughter who'd experienced abuse and was sympathetic toward Mark, especially when he brought the stolen items back to the store and asked how he could do restitution. Mark was re-hired as a sales person and was returned to his management position in six months.

TEEN COERCION

Giordano, Soto, Manning, and Longmore (2010) have suggested that abusive relationships among teenagers can be complex in that adolescents often experience conflicting and ambivalent feelings for their partners. The authors noted that programs should be open to and pay greater attention to teens when they express positive emotions surrounding their relationship. The presence of these positive feelings—ignored by many outreach programs—was an important reason why it was difficult for a teen to leave an abusive relationship.

Marcia

Marcia was flattered that Will chose her as his girlfriend. A football player and handsome teen, Will was nevertheless shy and lacked confidence. The fourth son in a family that emphasized sports, he was less successful than his three older brothers, and his ambitious father constantly criticized and even emotionally abused him. Witnessing his father hit, shove, and degrade his mother, Will was not sure what a healthy relationship with another would look like.

Marcia and her sister grew up with a mom and dad who were each mental health professionals—her mom was a social worker and her dad a psychiatrist. Receiving a lot of support and encouragement from her parents and her older sister, Marcia dreamed of becoming a pediatrician. She worked hard on her schoolwork and had a 4.0 grade point average. Already accepted at the college of her dreams, Marcia was enjoying having her first boyfriend, Will, although she had experienced the company of other boys who were her friends throughout high school.

Will, a senior at the same high school as Marcia, was seventeen years old. Marcia's seventeenth birthday was two weeks away when the incident occurred. Will had become critical of her and would put her down in front of others. When frustrated, he shoved her, once into the lockers, which was witnessed by others. His behavior became a matter of concern for Marcia, her parents, and the school counselor. But Will denied any problem, even when he drove too fast as part of an attempt to make Marcia comply with his request to attend a party in a dangerous part of town. They were on their way to attend the party and Marcia had changed her mind about going.

Will later reported that his speed had reached ninety-five miles an hour. When they arrived at the party, some teens were selling and using drugs, and there was plenty of alcohol available, mostly cans of beer and bottles of bourbon. Following Marcia around so she didn't call a taxi or her parents, Will told her that she must drink the punch, spiked with bourbon, and take some pills, which were a mixture of parents' medications stolen and mixed together by the youths. The party was raided by police because of the loud music and destruction of neighbors' property. Eggs were thrown at the windows of neighbors' houses and flowers were pulled up and thrown around yards. Vegetables and fruit ripening on a porch were stolen and thrown at trees.

Police arrested a large number of the teens, many of whom were drunk and belligerent. Marcia had refused to take the drugs and had only taken a few sips from one cup of the punch after Will shoved her into a tree. She was bruised on one side of her face and shoulder from being shoved. A police detective overheard Will threatening Marcia not to dare discuss anything about his driving or behavior at the party. The detective separated them and interviewed Marcia after her parents arrived. Marcia expressed fear about Will's speeding and shoving her roughly. She asked the detective how to make it up to the neighbors. Shortly afterward, Marcia's lawyer asked me to evaluate her.

> I was so scared. Will drove so fast, like ninety miles an hour. I thought I'd die in that car. He took away my cell. And he followed me around at the party. I wouldn't take much of a drink. And those pills. Who knew what they were? I wouldn't take any. So Will shoved me really hard. Right into a tree. My cheek and shoulder were bleeding. All those beautiful flowers. The kids ripped them up. I felt sorry for the woman next door. She came out of her house and cried. Her flowers were all over the place. I didn't know I could be part of that. Real meanness.

Psychosocial Evaluation
Marcia Lansom
Impact of Diagnosis on the Incident

Marcia was seen five times by her school counselor during the spring school term in 2012. The incident occurred after her fifth visit to Ms. Weilly, school counselor. Marcia had talked to Ms. Weilly about liking Will, but having concerns about how rough he would become, shoving and pushing her.

Counseling notes indicated concerns of Ms. Weilly after Marcia was seen with a black eye and bruises on her neck. However, Marcia would not admit that Will had caused these bruises. After consulting with the police department, Ms. Weilly had arranged for a joint conference at the school with Marcia, Will, their parents, the principal, and a police detective. This would have occurred the week after the incident in which Marcia and Will were arrested.

Captured by the Alion County Sheriff's Department, all of the students, including Marcia, were charged with underage drinking and destruction of property. Ms. Sandra Wells, a neighbor, reported during an interview with this evaluator that Marcia seemed upset when Ms. Wells's flowers had been pulled up; she heard Marcia yell at the others to leave her garden alone.

Will Myers agreed to be interviewed by this evaluator and, with his lawyer's permission, he admitted coercing Marcia into attending the party and shoving her hard into a tree to make her drink the bourbon-laced punch. Even then, Will told this evaluator, she only sipped a little; tests indicated that Marcia did not drink a significant amount of alcohol.

Will admitted being frightened that he would lose her when she left for college. So he followed, stalked, and surveilled Marcia at the party and other times, as well.

Marcia discussed with this evaluator her love, yet fear of her boyfriend, Will. She related numerous thoughtful and loving things that Will had shared with her. Marcia reported Will's fear of losing her and his growing violence as the time for her going away to college drew nearer. She was planning to attend a summer program at her new college.

Marcia experienced trauma and fear because of the dangerous situations in which Will had placed her, such as speeding in the car and exposure to mixed medications. As a young teen, Marcia did not know how to extricate herself from the situation. She described loving Will and appreciating his many kindnesses, like bringing her flowers and telling her she was pretty. Although she did not participate in destroying property, she expressed (to this evaluator) remorse and has joined with some other students in planting flowers in the yard of Ms. Wells. The group of seven students, led by Marcia, also brought groceries to an older neighbor, Ms. Tyson, whose fruit had been taken off the porch and smashed.

Marcia has already begun restitution on her own. She would appreciate additional opportunities to help in the community.

Diagnosis

As mentioned earlier, in a psychosocial evaluation, a specific diagnosis can be used, but in some cases, it may be less helpful than a description of how feelings, symptoms, and experiences contributed to someone's participation in an incident. Of course, if behavior involved no concern for others and there were no mitigating factors, this needs to be recognized as well. Marcia's efforts at restitution were allowed to be her only punishment.

Teen Violence Programs

There was an emphasis on negative and abusive behaviors in the program dealing with teen violence in Marcia's county. Marcia explained that she had seen the program's advertisements on television and on posters around school and her town. She didn't think it applied to her and Will because there was so much positive and fun in their relationship. Marcia did not believe that Will shoving and following her around had been frequent or a major part of their relationship.

ELDER COERCION

Coercion of older men and women is a nationwide concern. The types of abuse are multiple: financial, sexual, emotional, and physical. Research by the United States Department of Justice recommended that a broader approach be taken in regard to understanding elder abuse. The stress placed on the caregiver is currently seen as the primary cause of elder abuse, but other factors need to be considered to gain a full understanding.

> The response to elder maltreatment needs to change from a relatively fragmented approach unguided by theory to one that embraces a systematic approach drawn from a greater understanding of the underlying phenomenon. Further, these theories should take into account the characteristics of both the elderly victims and the abusive individuals, including their cognitive statuses, the nature of their relationships, the settings in which the abuse occurs, the type of abuse involved, and protective factors; in general, the theories should employ a more dynamic approach. (U.S. Department of Justice, 2013, p. 23)

Financial coercion is a process in which there is a threat or actual behavior involving the theft of money or goods; or the money/property may be used in ways not wanted or chosen by the older person. The coercer can be one person or a group, whether family members or external fraudulent others. In the interests of describing intimate coercion, the focus here will involve the financial coercion of older individuals by an intimate other—partner, child, sibling, or relatives.

Leslie

Leslie is an eighty-four-year-old woman who had amassed a fortune during her lifetime as a result of marriage to a wealthy man, keen investment skills, and earnings as the owner of a small business. She had a living trust that designated her monthly need for money, as well as a specified amount for each of her three children, now adults; there was an extra allowance for any child experiencing an emergency.

Her only son, Lanny, was a drug addict, and after using up his monthly allowance he would ask for additional funds for various emergencies, although other family members believed that he used the money to buy drugs. After several years, Leslie's lawyer suggested cutting off her son's monthly allowance to prevent him from using it for drugs. She was unwilling to do this, anticipating that he would become angry.

Her son moved into Leslie's home, against her two daughters' wishes. Each daughter was married and living elsewhere. Lanny began isolating their mother. A neighbor called both sisters, describing Lanny's yelling at Leslie, the noise so loud they could hear it from their porches and back yards.

When both sisters arrived for a visit, there was little food in the refrigerator. It was nearly supper time and, when asked, Leslie said she had eaten nothing yet that day.

Leslie had given four paintings to her daughters, two for each. While each had received the papers of ownership, they preferred to leave the paintings where Leslie would continue enjoying them. Her will provided that they would receive the paintings after her death. Yet, during the visit, her daughters observed that those four valuable paintings were missing from the walls.

When they asked their mother about the missing paintings and the bare wall, Leslie seemed nervous and unwilling to explain. Although usually very cheerful and active in clubs, Leslie appeared depressed and anxious.

Lanny arrived at Leslie's home later that day, and his sisters questioned him. He denied any knowledge about the missing paintings. The police were called by her daughters. During an interview with a detective, Leslie told him that she sold the paintings. Leslie kept looking across the room at Lanny, who was nodding and seemed to coach her in a threatening manner, pointing his finger at Leslie and shaking his head. He spoke to her in an irritated and angry tone of voice, asking if she didn't remember selling each of the paintings.

When the detective asked why she would sell paintings that belonged to her daughters, Leslie cried. Lanny laughed and the detective separated them, interviewing Leslie while another officer talked with Lanny in a separate room. It was then discovered that Lanny had sold the paintings for money to buy drugs. Leslie had been aware of this and was able to tell the detective when alone in the room with him, also explaining that Lanny threatened to leave her without food, take the telephones and her car, and leave her alone to starve. She believed these threats, although her daughters later wondered why Leslie didn't tell them or the neighbors. Leslie's lawyer asked for her to be evaluated, since Leslie seemed to have participated in theft of the paintings from her daughters, and she kept the sales a secret. During the evaluation, Leslie expressed sadness and fear of her son. "He said I'd starve if I told anyone about the paintings. It seems silly now that I think about it, but I believed him the last few weeks. His eyes get a wild look when he takes drugs. He raises his hand like he'll punch me. I pull back because I believe he'd do it."

> Psychosocial Evaluation
> Leslie Weinstock
> Impact of Diagnosis on the Incident

Suffering from trauma and depression, eighty-three-year-old Leslie Weinstock changed from a cheerful gardener and friendly neighbor to an isolated and frightened woman after her son moved into her house. Neighbors interviewed by this evaluator heard Lanny, her son, yelling at her; they called her two daughters to alert them.

Ms. Weinstock became aware of the sale of her daughters' paintings afterward. When she asked her son what had happened to them, he told her he'd sold the paintings and would starve and hurt her if she told anyone. He would raise his hand in the air as if delivering a slap, then stop and laugh at her. Fearful of harm from Lanny, she did not reveal this information to her daughters or the police. Her trauma includes such symptoms as fearfulness, anxiety, and flashbacks (to her son raising his hand as if to hit her).

Neighbors interviewed by this evaluator confirmed hearing yelling inside the house and in the backyard: Lanny shouted at his mother about a variety of things and one neighbor saw him raise his fist, but he didn't hit her. Glad to be interviewed, the neighbors on both sides of Leslie's home and across the street are two older women and a couple in their eighties. All expressed fear of Lanny who drove fast while drinking beer and throwing the bottles around the neighborhood. He had temper outbursts toward the newspaper delivery boy, a neighbor's wandering dog, and a variety of others. The neighbors expressed sorrow that their fear had kept them from calling the police.

Ms. Weinstock's fear of Lanny led to her silence about his sale of the paintings. Feeling sad and disappointed in her son, she stayed in her room most of the time, trying to avoid thoughts about her dilemma. She has experienced emotional and financial abuse by her son. Ms. Weinstock was deprived of food and threatened with being hit, leading to trauma and terror which she tried to cope with through her silence about the sale of the paintings.

An Understanding System

After police interviews with Ms. Weinstock and consideration of the psychosocial evaluation, there were no charges filed against her for illegal behavior. A judge issued a restraining order demanding that her son stay away from the house. Lanny came back to her home and was arrested once more when Ms. Weinstock and the neighbors called police. After that, Lanny moved to another area of the country. The paintings were recovered from a dealer where Lanny had taken them to be sold.

COERCION AND PEOPLE WITH DISABILITIES

Daniel had been injured in the army while fighting in Iraq. He was unable to walk due to a spinal cord injury and used a powered wheelchair. Daniel met Millie in an Internet chat room. She had been involved in a car accident as a child, resulting in a spinal cord injury: She also used a powered wheelchair when moving around or traveling. Each had a specially designed van and could travel and do errands independently. They lived in neighboring states and, after a few visits back and forth, Daniel and Millie became engaged. Shortly afterward they married and both families were hopeful for their future. Daniel was handsome with a good sense of humor and Millie was attractive and bright. She struggled with depression and took medicine to help stabilize her moods.

Millie moved into Daniel's wheelchair-accessible house and all seemed to be going well for several months. Others were unaware of Daniel's diagnosis of posttraumatic stress disorder (PTSD) by the Veterans Administration Hospital. After several months together, his outbursts included throwing things such as lamps and telephones at Millie. She was once treated at a hospital emergency room for bruises on her face and a cut on her neck, both resulting from Daniel throwing a telephone at her. Millie told the doctors that she had fallen down. Unfortunately, Daniel was allowed to remain in the room when doctors and nurses interviewed Millie, so she was afraid to tell them the truth.

Daniel shoplifted often, usually taking ties, wallets, and jewelry. Millie was surprised when she observed him in a store. He slipped a man's watch into his pocket. After the shoplifting incident that caused their arrests, Daniel told police that shoplifting seemed to lift his spirits. According to Millie and Daniel, both interviewed numerous times by this evaluator, Millie didn't like to shoplift and felt it was against her values. But she participated in the theft when Daniel threatened her on the day of their arrest. He threatened to leave Millie and put her out of his house if she did not allow him to put a stolen item in her purse. Since Daniel's name was on the house deed, and his disability check was their primary support, Millie was frightened of his threat. While she received a small disability check, it was not enough to support her. After giving up her low-rent apartment and part-time job to come live with Daniel, Millie felt vulnerable and concerned about her own survival.

Following Daniel's orders during the incident, she allowed him to slip two scarves into her purse while they shopped together. He took some wallets and covered them with the backpack on his lap. Both were caught, searched, and arrested.

Millie's lawyer asked me to evaluate her, and she talked with me about her shattered trust and sense of hopelessness.

> I haven't ever had a serious boyfriend before, kind of strange for a twenty-seven year old. But I really love Daniel. I was scared when he threatened to leave me. I believed him. But I shouldn't have done what I didn't believe in. I don't feel any hope. I thought I could trust him.

After the arrest, Millie's depression deepened and her medication was adjusted. Her parents posted bond and were allowed to bring Millie to their nearby home until her sentencing.

For Millie, like many of the coerced, the threat of abandonment caused fear that propelled her toward obeying orders that ran counter to a dearly held value system: Millie valued honesty and being trustworthy. Her disability made survival challenging, especially managing financially and maintaining independence. Millie's return to her parents' home was a sad occasion for her because of the family violence she had witnessed there as a child. She expected to witness it once again and was correct: Her father was still hitting and shoving her mother, as well as demeaning Millie.

> Psychosocial Evaluation
> Millie Pearson
> Impact of Diagnosis on the Incident

Newton Family Service Center records indicated that Millie, a twenty-seven-year-old disabled woman, was diagnosed with a depressive disorder and posttraumatic stress disorder six months prior to the theft. She was given psychotropic medication to help with high anxiety and panic attacks. Therapy notes described increased anxiety and a higher frequency of panic attacks after her marriage when there were reports of emotional abuse by Daniel: She reported his threats to make her leave the house and to end their marriage. A telephone interview by this evaluator with her therapist, as well as weekly therapy session notes, revealed that Millie had shared her observations of Daniel's shoplifting and his pressuring her to join him in the illegal activity.

Millie told this evaluator that she felt frightened the morning of the incident. She remembered him threatening to "kick me out of the house and divorce me" just before he ordered her to open her purse so he could stuff in the stolen scarfs. She also remembered crying and feeling a sense of panic, with difficulty breathing, typical of her panic attacks. Millie felt dizzy and frightened during the incident.

When the store detective approached them, Daniel escaped while Millie apologized, handing him the scarves. A policeman apprehended Daniel and both were arrested. Daniel told the detective that Millie had placed the scarves in her purse. Store video showed him taking the scarfs.

Fearful of Daniel's threats to abandon her and eject Millie from the house, she was coerced into taking the scarves. Millie's behavior was ordered by Daniel, who had been increasingly threatening and harmful during his rages. Hospital records from Lawton Medical Center described injuries to Millie during one of his rages. Neighbors heard him yelling orders at her and occasionally crashing furniture and lamps, which the husband and wife next door (Peter and Wendy Peterson) saw him throwing at her. Through open windows, and once in the backyard, they witnessed his orders, her obedience, or—if she seemed reluctant—his rageful behavior.

Regretful about the theft, Millie suggested restitution where she reimburses the store for the scarfs. In addition, she'd like to divorce Daniel and search for a part-time job and low-cost apartment, in order to help her recover her independence. She has been involved in therapy where Millie was helped to understand her behavior. Millie attends church where she reports seeing opportunities to make new friends.

Vulnerability among Disabled Persons

People with disabilities can be vulnerable in regard to struggles for independence, as well as experiencing trauma from illness and injuries. These are areas that coercers can prey upon. Isolation may be a problem for people with disabilities when more than average effort is required to interact with others (like having to use powered wheelchairs). There can be problems using shelters for people in wheelchairs, unless the shelters are equipped for disabilities.

COERCION OF CHURCH PARTNERS

Coercion by ministers and other church/temple leaders toward their partners often involves emotional abuse. Therapists and other health professionals need to be vigilant in watching for these women who suffer from emotional abuse and coercion that may isolate and frighten them. Their coercive experience often leads to various symptoms and feelings, such as physical (somatic) problems, depression, fearfulness, anxiety about obeying orders, anguish, and desperation.

Church coercion can take different forms, but a common experience is the use of authority (church, position, relationship to God) to claim the right to establish the "correct perception." This correct perception is the only one allowed, as in Biderman's Coercion Chart from Amnesty

International discussed previously (Biderman, 1973.) The woman's unique and different perception is often discounted, negated, ridiculed, criticized, and labeled in a negative way. While this emotional abuse is ongoing and continuous, warmth and crumbs of support are usually interspersed, confusing the coerced further, as with the intermittent re-inforcement noted previously in traumatic bonding (Dutton and Painter, 1993) and rare praise in Biderman's Coercion Chart (1973).

Tabitha

Tabitha was a vibrant and enthusiastic woman who married a minister from a church that was two hours away from her home in a rural area of a southern state. At first, she loved dressing in a more stylish way, as directed by her husband. He picked out her clothes and decided when and how many children they would have. He claimed that God spoke directly to him, governing his actions. Some of his directives included changes in Tabitha's behavior: She was to "quiet down" and become less enthusiastic, stay at home and begin having children, limit exposure to other people, and spend a great deal of time with the church finances and doing secretarial tasks for her husband, Pastor Charles.

Her family complained among themselves that her two sisters rarely saw or talked with Tabitha. Charles discouraged her parents from visiting since he kept Tabitha busy with church chores and having children in close succession. With their three children, Charles allowed brief visits to her parent's home for holidays. He was always by her side, monitoring discussions with family and friends. He made jokes about occasional bruises that her family noticed, especially on Tabitha's neck and face. He explained she was always bumping into things. Tabitha said little and seemed sad and withdrawn.

Charles was accused of sexual activity with underage girls. The sexual activity was found to have sometimes occurred in the church when Tabitha was doing work in the office. Both were arrested and charged with child abuse. Tabitha explained that she was not aware of his illegal behavior: "I was supposed to stay in the office and do the financial work and newsletter and whatever else he told me to do. I wasn't allowed to open the door. Charles said I could disturb church activities; once I asked how. He grabbed me by the neck and squeezed. Once I couldn't breathe and passed out. I did what he said."

Psychosocial Evaluation
Tabitha Chandler
Impact of Diagnosis on the Incident

Ms. Chandler's trauma resulted from her husband's continuous emotional abuse and coercion. His multiple orders for completion of tasks and child care left her exhausted and depressed. His threats and physical abuse, like choking, caused her fear and a sense of hopelessness. She felt helpless, seeing no way to avoid following his orders. He threatened to divorce her and take away their children if she did not obey him. Questioning him would lead to what he called, "God's punishment," which he administered by choking and slapping her.

Witnessed by three church members (interviewed by this evaluator), his choking would continue until she lost consciousness, even when Ms. Chandler was holding one of her three young children ranging in age from one to four years old. Fearful about harm to her children when they were dropped, or shoved against walls by her husband, she obeyed orders, including leaving the church office door closed and not exiting the room without his permission. He told church members that a radio was left playing loudly in the room to prevent outside noise from distracting whoever was working there.

This evaluator went to the church office with an investigator who played the same radio loudly. Voices could not be heard when someone was speaking a few rooms away, where the sexual activity was found to have occurred. This seemed consistent with the abused children's statements to the police; the children reported hearing loud music.

Mrs. Chandler reported that she was not aware of her husband's abuse toward children in the church. She now feels responsible for not having protected these children.

She is on suicide watch at the Marion County jail where her mental health diagnosis includes depression and anxiety, which are being treated with Elavil. Doctor Tim Samuels reported in his mental health notes that Ms. Chandler had difficulty sleeping, was not eating much at all, and was experiencing "such other trauma symptoms as flashbacks to being choked by her husband and dissociation." Dr. Samuels noted that he needed to touch her shoulder to get her attention when calling her name did not stop her staring into space.

During the abuse by her husband toward children in the church, Ms. Chandler was doing tasks that he had ordered her to perform, including deskwork and preparing the church bulletin. Unaware of her husband's illegal activities, she now feels remorse and despair that the children were seriously harmed.

Sentencing for Tabitha

Tabitha was given probation in a bench trial where the judge heard evidence, including her psychosocial evaluation and various witnesses testifying about the family violence. She became involved in therapy and moved to another location, reporting to a nearby probation officer. Her children were returned to her home.

INTIMATE COERCION TOWARD CHILDREN

Intimate coercion toward children can take many forms. The essence of intimate coercion involves forcing children into unwanted, uncomfortable, illegal, and/or harmful behavior in order to satisfy the adult's or older sibling's needs or wants. And the coercers can include parents, older siblings, cousins, neighbors, school mates, other family members, family friends, godparents, etc. When children are forced into unwanted and harmful behaviors, they learn their own needs and comfort are not important, respected, or valued. Rather, they see themselves being used, in order to fill others' wants.

Adam's Coercion by His Brother

Adam's older brother, Sam, bullied him without any constraint or correction from his parents, who often witnessed Sam's behaviors. Sam was twelve years old and Adam seven years old. Sam would shove Adam into walls, tear off his clothes and poor hot water on his behind and genitals, yell and call him names ("stupid," "dumb," "ugly"). Sam would order Adam to perform tasks, like shoplift packs of gum for Sam. While many brothers fight and argue, Sam's coercive behavior was continuous, as well as physically and emotionally abusive.

His parents heard Adam's screams occasionally and would go to his bedroom. Once Sam was shoving a brush down Adam's throat; on another occasion he was putting a hair brush handle into Adam's rectum. The parents went to a therapist with the children, but soon dropped out because the father was too embarrassed to discuss Sam's behaviors. They did not tell the therapist about the bullying and abuse.

The boys' school was broken into and two computers were stolen. Sam told other students that Adam was the thief. When a teacher heard the accusation about Adam's theft, she reported it to the principal, who called police. Adam was taken out of class and arrested. He admitted his part in the theft, but refused to tell the police who else was involved.

Adam's lawyer noticed his fearfulness and asked for a psychosocial evaluation. Adam, as well as family members, teachers, and neighbors were interviewed. Loring suggested that Adam have a psychological evaluation because school testing showed some hyperactive behaviors and difficulty doing math problems. She also recommended an examination by a psychiatrist, since the family doctor had prescribed medication for anxiety. Loring's family history and collateral witness interviews were shared with the psychologist and psychiatrist who also evaluated him.

Adam asked not to be let out of juvenile detention; he did not want bond paid that would allow him to return home. He explained to Loring: "I feel safe here. And people are really nice to me. And the food is good. We get popcorn at night. And I get to say what television I like to watch. No one yells at me. Or hurts me. I like it here."

Psychosocial Evaluation
Adam Crenson
Impact of Diagnosis on the Incident

As a young child (seven years old), Adam has been recently diagnosed by Dr. Susan Benson with posttraumatic stress disorder. He was given medication to help with anxiety and sleeplessness. Adam exhibited trauma symptoms during his interview with this evaluator. He cried a great deal and would shake with anxiety while recounting the abuse he experienced at the hands of his brother, Sam. Adam explained to this evaluator that he did what Sam said, so he (Adam) wouldn't get "beat up" and "talked bad to." Adam stared into space and explained that he sometimes couldn't concentrate in school classes, having flashbacks to Sam's pouring hot water on his genitals and shoving objects into his rectum. He was frightened each day about what would happen to him that evening.

Feeling unprotected by his parents, Adam told a favorite teacher about his brother's behavior. The teacher reported this to child protective services three different times, but home visits (2) did not result in any action.

Adam was unwilling to discuss the school theft. When this evaluator asked what he'd like to become, Adam quickly said he planned to be a journalist and artist. Invited by this evaluator to write an article about the theft and to draw sketches of the theft, Adam depicted with bright crayon colors the theft in which one figure forced another figure to break a window with an ax and climb into a classroom, removing two computers stored in a closet. Adam painted a red strip on the figure's back, where "my brother made a cut with the ax on my back and said that he would chop off my head if I didn't do what he said." A similar theme emerged when this evaluator asked Adam to write a newspaper article about the theft.

This evaluator requested that the juvenile detention center nurse come into the interview room and, with Adam's permission, Adam's back was examined. There was an untreated wound running from one shoulder to his lower back. A scab had recently formed. The nurse suggested that the scratch be photographed (please see attached photograph of Adam's back, signed by nurse Peggy Wilson).

Adam did participate in the school theft after being threatened and cut by his brother, Sam, who coerced Adam previously and at the time of the incident. Adam expressed sorrow for the theft of two computers from the classroom of "my very favorite teacher." He asked this evaluator to protect him so that he wouldn't do "any more bad things that my brother makes me do." Adam discussed his brother's harm to animals, including their own family dog. Adam was forced to watch some of these injuries occur, and "I can't stop thinking about them." Coercion by his brother led to the school theft in which Adam reluctantly participated.

Neighbors, other students, teachers, and the grandmother and grandfather all described (to this evaluator) bullying and coercion by Sam toward Adam. Most of them had talked with the parents, asking them to attend to the problem to protect Adam. None of them were aware of any protective actions taken for Adam.

Adam's Brighter Future

Please note that the three items mentioned in the evaluation were attached to the psychosocial evaluation, but are not included in this book: A drawing of the theft by Adam, a newspaper article that Adam wrote about the theft, and the picture of Adam's back wound. (Confidentiality of the child was protected in this way.)

There was some deficit in his math abilities discovered by the psychologist and a math tutor was found to help Adam. The psychiatrist diagnosed Adam with PTSD and changed his medication; Adam reported feeling much better. On occasion, it is helpful to have additional evaluations by a psychiatrist specializing in trauma, medication, and neurological issues; in some cases, it is important to have help from a psychologist knowledgeable about IQ, hyperactivity, learning disabilities, neurological issues, control, coercion, and violence. There are additional professionals skillful in many areas of family dynamics and development, trauma, and coercion, including counselors, family therapists, social workers, nurses, and others.

Adam moved to his favorite aunt's home, because the court suggested that he live separately from his brother. There were no legal consequences for Adam's illegal behavior. Adam enjoyed being the only child in his aunt's home and made many friends. At his new school, he started a student newspaper where he could report on important events. He also created drawings that were published in the newspaper. Adam made straight A's and was now the publisher of a newspaper, with support from other students and teachers. His medication for anxiety was stopped, and Adam wrote Loring a letter to describe his happiness; he included a copy of the newspaper, as well.

10

Transformation of the Coerced

Mayerhof (1971) has explored the process of caring where encouragement from another inspires a person to trust herself. Her growth brings forth admiration and delight among those caring for her: She feels assured by this caring—she is not alone. Many of the coerced experience loneliness in the absence of this caring. During transformation, their healing involves seeking caring and comfort from others.

The coerced are traumatized in ways that are similar to other trauma victims, as well as ways that are unique to the coercion process. Those professionals helping the coerced to transform their lives need to be familiar with theory about abuse, trauma, and coercion, as well as the profound struggle for connection among the abused: An excellent source is Herman's book on trauma and recovery (1997). Specific issues relating to coercion must be identified, analyzed, and understood not only by the therapist, but also by the coerced. Sharing information, support, and options with the coerced allows them to recall and embrace the sense of self, as well as grow in new and exciting directions.

CONNECTION FOR THE TRAUMATIZED

Herman suggests group therapy as an effective way to treat the traumatized.

> Traumatic events destroy the sustaining bonds between individual and community. Those who have survived learn that their sense of self, of worth, of humanity, depends upon a feeling of connection to others. The solidarity of

a group provides the strongest protection against terror and despair, and the strongest antidote to trauma experience. Trauma isolates; the group re-creates a sense of belongingness. Trauma shames and stigmatizes; the group bears witness and affirms. Trauma degrades the victim; the group exalts her. Trauma dehumanizes the victim; the group restores her humanity. (1997, p. 214)

Connection with others who reach out with caring protection helps combat the terror and anxiety that envelope the coerced. To feel a sense of belonging comforts many coercion victims who feel isolated. And affirmation from caring others can ease the self-doubt and struggles among those experiencing coercion.

Another path to healing involves individual therapy that focuses on connection, integration, self-forgiveness, reestablishing the self, and community involvement. With the coerced, there is initially a need for individual therapy, since they often experience profound shame, embarrassment, and stigma that could be overwhelming to share in a group; many of the coerced do not initially feel able to expose themselves to others while coping with the horror of their participation in sad and/or horrific crimes. Having violated personal values and their sense of morality, the coerced must seek self-compassion and self-forgiveness before hoping for the acceptance and forgiveness of others. And forgiving oneself is a tremendous struggle for those whose coercion has led to illegal behaviors that are not in keeping with their own value system.

Steele has suggested that "so many of my patients do not accept the concept of forgiveness, but they can become compassionate" (personal interview with Kathy Steele, February 9, 2015). Many therapists, Loring included, envision a hope for healing in which the coerced discover greater kindness, gentleness, and compassion toward themselves while looking into the mirror of a compassionate therapist/intervening helper, as well as others who support her new adventures.

The denial and dissociation experienced by many of the coerced may leave them unable to be attentive and emotionally present during group therapy. For Steele, groups are a "powerful shame-buster" (personal interview with Kathy Steele, February 9, 2015). However, she has concerns about group therapy for those who are dissociative "until they have learned more effective skills to cope with their tendency to avoid emotions and reality. Otherwise, they can become too easily overwhelmed with emotions they cannot yet handle" (personal interview with Kathy Steele, February 9, 2015).

TRANSFORMATION OF THE COERCED

The Remnants of Coercion

How can a peace-loving, gentle person make sense of the evidence that she has participated in making a bomb used to harm others? How can a coerced woman feel honest when she has participated in a bank robbery, bank fraud, or stock fraud? How can she live with herself when her beloved pet has been harmed?

The coerced feel guilty and sad, filled with anguish, horrified at a "loved one's" betrayal, embarrassed and humiliated, distrustful of her own judgment, and lost in relation to who she is in the community, which might be angry and judgmental of her. It is not like a natural disaster. No one, including herself, initially sees the coerced as an innocent victim, especially when she has played a part in a crime, even a tragedy. Transformational therapy must help her cope with guilt and humiliation, as well as assist her rediscovery of self-trust.

Considerations for Therapists and Other Change Agents

The transformation of a coerced person is an exciting process. It is important for therapists and other change agents to understand fragmentation of the self. For the coerced, therapy is not helpful when a therapist (or other change agent) embraces an expectation of ending "co-dependence" by trying to immediately separate the woman from her abuser. This is not possible when the coerced has no put-together sense of self with which to separate. The initial goal should involve identifying fragmented pieces of the self. This is a relational process. That is, the coerced person relates to her therapist, who is encouraging, validating, and a partner in recovery of the self. The coerced can then relate to people, groups, activities, and causes that illuminate the shadows of the emerging self (Loring, 1994). The coerced struggle to envision who she was and who she can become; for her to emerge from the shame and horror, she must see the possibility of finding meaning in her horrific experiences. It is this hope that escorts her from futility and hopelessness.

Numbing in the coerced person should not be mistaken for another type of diagnosis. Paralyzed with fear and overwhelmed with shame, the coerced can appear emotionless. As suggested by Kaufman, some problems with diagnosis are caused by her numbing that can be misperceived as a lack of caring, guilt, or remorse. Yet, often the guilt and remorse among coerced women is profound (G. Kaufman, personal communications, June 18, 2014).

SYDNEY WAS CAUGHT IN HER HUSBAND'S FRAUD

Coercion is ongoing and does not necessarily stop, even after the arrest, when both the coerced and community members react to the crime. In Sydney's case, the community was furious at her coercive husband, who defrauded them through an elaborate investment scheme. Many lost their life savings and children's college funds. Sydney consistently denied knowing the fraudulent nature of the scheme. Yet, many had been brought into the financial plan through her excitement and hope; they blamed her for their losses.

Sydney was diagnosed as depressed by a mental health professional in jail. Her hesitance to believe the crime and numbed appearance were diagnosed as sociopathic—denying and uncaring about the crime. The depression improved and her denial stopped after she saw evidence of his fraudulent behavior. She developed a plan to pay victims back their savings. Sydney set up a restitution fund with a local bank handling all transactions and sought contributions from corporations for the victims.

After this effort and court testimony about her abuse, many community members began to see her in a different way. Court testimony included witnesses, medical records, and the psychosocial evaluation; information revealed sexual, emotional, and physical abuse that had been used to coerce her into following orders. After hearing the testimony, Sydney understood more about her husband's fraudulent behavior and how he had coerced her into participating. With decreasing traumatic shock, she was able to express her regret and remorse with genuine feeling.

I know everyone thinks I meant to steal from them. I didn't know. I thought it would be a great way they'd make money with his investment scheme. My husband would throw me down the stairs and against walls. He forced me to watch porno videos. He was nicer when I helped him get contributors. But he wasn't investing money. I found out later he spent it. And as fast as it came in. I felt too ashamed to talk with anyone.

TRANSFORMATIONAL TASKS FOR THE THERAPIST AND INTERVENER

During intervention and therapy, the first thing the coerced woman should notice is a deep respect from her therapist or advocate: Whatever the coerced woman says or feels is accepted and even validated as a normal and understandable idea, feeling, wish, or hope. Coerced people need to experience a language of honor and acceptance. The "mutuality" described in literature from the Stone Center captures this honoring of another's perceptions, as well as caring about the needs of the other, where there is respect for both peoples' ideas in a relationship. To be heard with empathy, respect, and interest—what a different experience for a coerced woman who has been criticized, labeled, discounted, and coerced into obedience without regard for her needs.

Wholeness of the coerced's self begins to develop in relation to this caring other person—the therapist or advocate—during the experience of being heard, understood, and validated. Validation comes in many forms, but its essence is acceptance and positive feedback: "Yes, I can understand your feeling that way"; "What a great idea"; "I am interested in hearing more about that." Some therapists are comfortable with self-disclosure, sharing that the therapist had a similar experience or feeling. This can be an important way to help a coerced woman find her way back to feeling normal.

While the coercer's orders and the coerced person's subsequent behavior might add up to a harmful whole, the coerced woman needs help in traveling past her own limited view. As has been discussed, she has often seen the pieces of the project without understanding the ultimate purpose. She feels frightened in the darkness of confusion. This tunnel vision involves hearing immediate orders and seeing only her part of a project or event. When the coerced hears a cognitive explanation for her limited vision and blindness to the ultimate plan, she can move closer to forgiving herself.

Because she has experienced the covert emotional abuse of projection ("It is all your fault," says the coercer) and denial ("And I have done nothing at all," also from the coercer), she is quick to blame herself for any horror committed. After understanding these mechanisms of coercion, women who have been coerced often express amazement and sometimes describe their shoulders as feeling lighter from less worry and weight pressing on them.

As the therapist clarifies who ordered what and which threats might have been carried out, the control and coercion are made clear to the coerced woman. Her confusion falls apart: She begins to see and understand ritualized abuse. She starts to recognize the coercive process that has stolen her sense of self and left her empty and confused in the midst of an abusive relationship where that is the goal—to empty and "disappear the self." The coercer's purpose is to make more room to shovel in orders, threats, and emotional abuse (Loring, 1994). Yet, often unaware of the source or ritualized nature of their suffering, the victim's cries for help are not always clear or loud enough to be heard—not by herself or others. Coerced women suffer "invisible wounds [that] can result in desperation, confusion, accidents, and even suicide" (Loring, 1994, p. 13).

Alicia Partnoy is a human rights activist and poet from Argentina. She is a survivor of a secret detention camp where many Argentineans disappeared, without their friends and families knowing their whereabouts. She described her own experiences as "a disappeared."

For the coerced woman, being emotionally "disappeared" is real and terrifying: Her sense of self is fragmented and disappeared from what it had been; others, including friends and family, experience her isolation and withdrawal as her having all but disappeared from them. Partnoy (1992) has written in her poetry that others say she speaks too softly, that she seems to be almost mumbling. They cannot hear her pain, which she thought was coming out in piercing screams.

To hear these silent, yet piercing screams of emotional pain and fear—this is a crucial task of intervention and therapy with the coerced. For the therapist to voice understanding and validate feelings, once ridiculed and disappeared, is the foundation on which transformation can take place in relation to the therapist and others.

11

Therapeutic Intervention with the Coerced

In her poem "Por/traits," Alicia Partnoy (2014) described brutal people as infrequent travelers on the guilt train, since they do not seek forgiveness, repentance, or absolution (2014). For the coerced woman, being in relationship with brutality makes her a frequent traveler on the guilt train; she is sad and full of anguish and self-blaming.

Therapeutic intervention must help the coerced regain her sense of self, escape from anguish and despair, and deal with guilt and shock about the results of her coerced behavior. The coercion process introduces other therapeutic needs, including a period of grieving, growing skills in forgiveness and self-compassion, and restoring lost hope; these form the GFH (grief, forgiveness, hope) triad, which is a crucial consideration for recovery to occur. Many of the coerced embrace feelings of relief and joy while exploring this triad and discovering possibilities for healing.

A coerced client may feel overcome and overwhelmed with feelings. Occasional dissociation can result in staring into space or similar behavior, and traumatic events may be reexperienced in the form of flashbacks. It can be valuable to remember the possible need for stabilization prior to treatment, as described earlier by Steele and her colleagues.

However, many of the coerced, feeling a growing sense of relief and safety, are eager to understand their experiences and explore new choices. Recognizing covert and ritualized emotional abuse during coercion brings clarity and a sense of hope. And many find comfort and even excitement in remembering and connecting lost parts of themselves that had been drowned in the abusive process. Relating to an encouraging therapist/intervener, the coerced explore new ways to live life's adventures. In relational connective intervention, developed by Loring, there are eight components.

EIGHT COMPONENTS OF
RELATIONAL CONNECTIVE INTERVENTION

There are eight essential components in working with the coerced:

1. therapeutic stance
2. therapeutic endeavor
3. therapeutic mode
4. rebuilding the self
5. clarification
6. grief and forgiveness
7. restoration of hope
8. transformation

Therapeutic Stance

Therapeutic stance is the therapist's (or other helper's) respect and encouragement for the woman's unfolding self. Searching for her strengths and interests, dreams and hopes, is an important part of therapy. The therapist helps her to explore groups that she would like to join, as well as causes where she could advocate for others whose plight touches her heart. This proceeds if the client wishes and at her own pace.

A coerced woman finds, with the therapist and during her own explorations, that there is hope for a different way of relating, where you are valued and known rather than ordered and threatened. Searching with the therapist for past and present strengths and connections, this is the model for moving forward in a transformative way. Looking back into her history can bring clarity to repeated patterns of being abused and coerced in relationships. Transformation involves a change in these patterns, an expectation of being treated in as kind a way as she is now learning to treat herself.

In the therapeutic stance, the therapist is an advocate for the coerced's hopes and dreams, which need to blossom up from under her shame and guilt. The therapist validates the client's feelings, ideas, and perceptions. The emotionally abused, coerced client, who wades through despair and anguish, desperately needs to feel valued and comforted by the therapist and, later, by herself. Only then will hope trickle back into her thoughts, feelings, and behavior.

Different therapists have different styles, but the goal is relational encouragement. Coerced people commonly are despairing and profoundly isolated, and the therapist helps such a person know perhaps "for the first time in life what it means to have someone on his side, an advocate" (Sakheim and Devine, 1992).

The exploration of coercive experiences may lead to pain; to take this "risk remembering," they must feel toward the therapist a sense of trust and partnership, emotional safety and comfort (Sakheim and Devine, 1992). Therapeutic connections are marked by the therapist's empathy and support so that the fragmented self begins to integrate in connection with another.

Some of the interventions described in chapter 2 can be helpful as part of the transformation. These techniques assist in treating trauma and encouraging recovery. Since trauma is such a large part of coercion, the focus on its treatment is valuable. At the same time, relational transformation is essential for learning new ways of relating and discovering lost dreams, while—at the same time—creating new hopes.

Mary's "Failure to Protect"

Mary believed Tony's repeated criticisms of her "poor" mothering. Their two young children were put to bed each night by Tony, who favored his obedient daughter and often yelled at their rebellious son. One night, when their son, Robbie, was refusing to go to bed, Tony dragged him to the bedroom and Mary heard a crash. Running into the room, she saw Robbie holding his arm and crying. Tony ordered her out and delivered his usual threat that, if she didn't obey, he'd take the children away from her "lousy" parenting and she'd never see them again. Looking back, Mary was not certain why she completely believed this threat, but thought it was because of Tony's power as an attorney in the community.

At parties and when they were interacting with others, Tony would laugh about "mistakes" he thought Mary had made raising the children. While he made up some of the stories, Mary laughed with Tony and others, afraid of his anger if she disputed the accuracy of his stories. He portrayed her as a naive or inept mother. Looking back, Mary realized Tony was surveilling her, watching her in the house and out in the community. While at the park with her children, she would see him peering at her from his car.

Each morning, Tony insisted on dressing the children and taking them to school in a hurried manner that only permitted Mary a quick kiss as they rushed out the door. The school nurse called Mary the day after Tony had been jerking his arm because Robbie's arm was hurting. Mary called Tony, but Mary was told by his secretary that Tony was too busy to talk with her. Mary went to the school, picked up Robbie, and took him to the pediatrician. Sent to the hospital, Mary discovered that Robbie's arm was broken, although the child seemed too frightened to explain what had happened.

Because of the mysterious circumstances, the hospital social worker called police. Tony told police by telephone that Mary had probably harmed Robbie. She was arrested and questioned. Later, when Robbie told police that his father had slammed him against the wall the night before, Tony was arrested. Mary's charges involved failure to protect her child. She was distraught about her son's injury.

> I'm horrified that I didn't protect Robbie. I was so scared Tony would take him away from me. I'm ashamed that I didn't know Robbie was being hurt. Everyone thought I was a bad mother, and so did I. So I stayed away when Tony told me to and let him care for the children.

Tony continued to blame Mary during the legal proceedings, but Robbie's input made Mary's coercion clear. The judge's sentence for Mary involved some brief jail time, then probation, parenting classes, and therapy. Eager for growth and hoping to become the best possible mother, Mary requested that Loring help her in therapy, where she grieved about and forgave herself for her son's injury. She also focused on her hope and dream of finishing college and attending law school.

Therapeutic Endeavor

Therapeutic endeavor is the heart of therapy with the coerced. It is an effort by the therapist and the coerced to understand together the basis of her anguish: How could she have participated in what many coerced consider an evil act without being evil herself? How could she have missed the larger crime while focused on the particulars? How could she have lost her self and become an obedient pawn to a loved one? The coerced wonder if they can trust again and they question whether to believe that someone will have their best interests at heart. And can they trust themselves when many encounter disdain, not only from their partner, but also from victims of a crime in which they have participated?

This endeavor is a matter for discussion between a therapist and the coerced. How can the therapist share comfort in the midst of the coerced's anguish? Is an arm around the shoulder comfortable for both the therapist and the coerced? If not, then what type of nonsexual and nonthreatening comfort works for both? Are there favorite objects whose presence brings peace to the coerced during therapy sessions when her anguish pours out? Would she find comfort during a brief intermission (during therapy sessions) to call and hear a loved one's voice? This kind of discussion about what brings comfort conveys the concern and respect of the therapist, as well as allows sharing of control with someone who has submitted to another's control. The coerced often reflect joy and hope with this kind of endeavor, learning ways to comfort themselves, as well as creating the climate for the process of clarification (discussed later).

Myra's "Insider Information"

Revealing insider information from her company, Myra told her husband, a stockbroker, about her company's planned growth. His threats to leave her played a large part in her illegal behavior. When he ordered Myra to use a disguised name and buy stock in her company, she obeyed. Later, she was charged with insider trading and sentenced to a year in prison.

After her release from prison, Myra requested therapy with Loring. Myra grieved about her loss of respect in the community, as well as for not adhering to her own values and for the likely end of her career as executive of a company. Myra's anger and unforgiving disgust with herself were important in her therapeutic work. She expressed her awareness of our endeavor and occasionally took breaks during therapy to call a cousin who was supportive and encouraging. Myra began to feel more hopeful and explored ways to share her knowledge with the community.

> I feel your respect and I'm beginning to respect myself. And I'm protecting myself from people who'd use me. I'm giving talks at clubs about holding on to values. And I talked about my experience at my company's annual meeting. The president of the company told me I could work again under supervision. Imagine that!

Therapeutic Mode

The therapeutic mode blends the coerced woman's movement away from trauma and toward new styles of attachment. As part of the therapeutic mode, a therapist validates the woman's experience with terror, with making choices that would result in the least possible harm to herself and others. At the same time, the coerced is invited to search, if she wishes, for joyful experiences with meaning, even while coping with trauma and profound sadness. At the pace of the coerced, not the therapist, these invitations can be accepted with a slowly growing sense of disattachment from the coercer and the coercive process, while creating new styles of attachment.

Disattachment is the beginning of withdrawal from the coercive process. Less time is spent remembering and experiencing flashbacks about aspects of the coercion and crime. There is a growing gentleness in the coerced's self-blame, more understanding of the coercive process, and development of creative ways to cope with guilt, regret, and sadness about the crime(s), including attempts to help others. She may witness different parts of the self returning, even developing.

The coerced person is beginning to move from the all-consuming experience of drowning in the coercive process. Coming up for air, she is looking around to see who will betray and harm her. During this beginning disattachment, the coerced sees and cares about her self in a process of reintegration. A therapist's affirmation nourishes the coerced, helps to gather the fragmented parts of her self. The therapist is a mirror reflecting hope. Disattachment can only continue when the coerced begins to feel a sense of identity. While filling in a sense of who she is, the coerced begins to separate from the coercer and the coercive process.

Rebuilding the Self

A therapist can help the coerced woman remember the lost parts of her self and discuss—even name—new parts. This is a helpful way to regrow oneself. "Adventurer," "advocate" (against drunk driving), "writer," are some self parts that coerced clients have remembered and created while engaged in therapy. Rebuilding the self is reestablishing what coercion has not destroyed, but crumbled. The self lies in disarray, disappeared from its original form. For some, naming those rediscovered or newly created parts is fun and makes them seem real and alive. For others, naming is not as important as simply recognizing them, often in the context of such hobbies as writing and causes that are heartfelt.

The coerced will look over her shoulder for the coercer's surveillance and hear his orders in her head, traumatized and terrified even after separation from him. When she feels safer, knowing her loved ones are also free from threat and harm, then this integrative connective therapy can increase her trust and sense of adventure in relating to others, joining groups, and supporting causes. Some of the coerced move quickly into disattachment from the coercive partner and begin reconnections with others, especially causes and groups. Others may prefer developing skills where they can work by themselves primarily, like writing articles for a county newspaper or just for fun. Some initially stay with the coercer while maintaining safety and setting limits that allow for their growth and reintegration of the self. Therapy is important in making a transformative change from a coerced to a reconnected and integrated person.

Clarification

Many of these processes blend together while working with the coerced, who must—with the therapist's clarifications—develop a clear understanding of the coercive dynamics she experienced. So profound is her confusion that clarification helps her understand, even forgive herself, for what Kaufman called "her abhorrent behavior," since she is heartbroken about her own coerced acts (G. Kauffman, personal communications, June 18, 2014).

Anne's Betrayal

Not all coercion results in illegal behavior. Anne's new husband, Jake, threatened to harm her dog, a collie named Prince, by letting it go out into the neighborhood with no leash, or turn him loose on some country road where the dog couldn't find a route home. The only way to prevent this, according to Jake, was for Anne to give him her undivided attention. Sometimes he said nothing, just looked annoyed at her dog, and Anne thought the looks were hidden threats. He objected to Anne visiting her parents in a nearby town. She answered her parents' telephone calls but was often interrupted with demands from Jake. He decided they were too busy to visit her parents. Jake ordered her to come directly home from work and he supervised her behavior, using her as his legal secretary to do chores for him. Finally, Jake insisted that she quit her job as a realtor and work full-time in his law firm. Anne came to therapy with Loring when she experienced repeated chest pains: Numerous medical tests failed to reveal a cause.

Anne believed that she'd "lost" herself "somewhere" during the year she'd been married to Jake. She searched for the self she had once liked. Together with the therapist, Anne searched for and named her parts, both old lost ones and new, as well.

> I wanted to name my parts to remember who I'd been. Then I thought of some new parts and began to get excited about recalling the old and creating some new parts for myself. Life seemed full of promise. I hid my dog at an old friend's home and moved in with my parents, who were thrilled. Let's see, there's "the traveler" who wants to take a course at a university in London and "the daughter" who wants to be kind to her parents. Then "little me" loves to eat out after each house I sell. I love being a realtor again and I joined a sculpture class, so "the artist" makes great statues. I feel safe and full of ideas that no one can take away from me anymore. And no one can hurt my dog. I don't have chest pains now; maybe my heart was breaking.

It seems to observers that the coerced ought to have recognized the manipulation and threats of the coercer. She may recall some, but coercion can involve threats and ritualized abuse that are covert and hidden. Clarification is valuable for the coerced, especially when the therapist helps her to analyze the elements of coercion. For Anne, this would include threats (to harm her dog), her feelings (fear), and symptoms (anxiety and chest pains). A structure developed by Loring to clarify the coercive experience is the Coercive Abuse Climate Map (see table 11.1). This tool maps

Table 11.1.　The Coercive Abuse Climate Map

Type of Coercion	Coercive Tool	Demand	Response	1) Consequences 2) Feelings 3) Symptoms

out the coercive behavior as a climate the coerced is living in and depicts her feelings, symptoms, and reactive behaviors.

A therapist can help the coerced map out the climate, including the type of coercion (threats), coercive tools (like ritualized emotional abuse), demand (mail this box), response (obeyed), consequences (bomb mailed, man harmed), feelings (terror), symptoms (can't sleep, eat, concentrate; chest pains and headaches). This method of clarification can help the coerced understand her anxiety and terror, normal reactions to her experiences.

Using this tool can normalize responses to the coerced behavior while encouraging compassion and understanding. Hearing a therapist acknowledge the horror of threats to harm children and animals, as well as the torturous obedience to protect them, adds a new perspective and clarity for the coerced who may, for the first time, recognize her impossible choices and courage in protecting, as best she could, those she loves. Only then will compassion and forgiveness be possible.

Depth is added to this clarification by the therapist asking when else the coerced might have experienced any of this. Sometimes the coercion is a mirror of childhood experiences, perhaps with a bully, parents, siblings, neighbors, relatives, and/or friends. A separate coercive map(s) can provide additional understanding of these past experiences. The coerced will begin to see patterns in her life, as well as recognizing new ways to connect.

Susan's Dangerous and Coerced Driving Experiences

Susan's coercion involved her husband, Ivan, who demanded that she accompany him to bars where he would have several drinks, then insist on driving home. He drove too fast and sometimes looked away from the road. Whenever Susan asked for safer driving, he discounted her fears, saying she was too anxious for no reason. The few times she refused to get into the car with him, he threatened to kill her. Since Ivan had choked her once, this threat seemed real to her. Once she refused to get into the car and the day after her refusal, he bought a gun and waved it around in front of her. During a wild ride when Ivan was driving, he crossed the line dividing lanes and hit another car, killing the driver. While there were no charges against Susan, she felt partly responsible for the death."It's something I will always remember and see in my mind, over and over. I'll always wish I had stolen his keys and run away."

Susan was initially arrested, then released. During therapy begun after her release, she was helped to complete a coercive abuse climate map (see table 11.2). The types of coercion experienced by Susan were threats to kill her and his drunk driving with her as a passenger. Coercive tools were unsafe driving, threats, and discounting her fear. The demand was forced danger, to ride with him during unsafe driving, and the response was that she obeyed. Tragically, the consequence was that a man was killed. Susan felt horrified, guilty, sad, and depressed; she was unable to sleep and struggled with anxiety and headaches.

After arrest, the coercer and the coerced may both get out of jail on bond. It is important to remember that conducting this type of therapy, while the coerced is still attached to the coercive partner (married, living with, dating), can bring danger to someone already threatened with harm. Some battered women are harmed or killed upon leaving the relationship, so helping a physically abused, coerced woman gain independence could persuade her to leave the relationship, leading to possible harm. Safety is an important consideration for the coerced and for the therapist. And yes, therapists and advocates must take care of their own safety issues in these situations.

Clarification is essential to clear up confusion and rebuild the self. During clarification and rebuilding, growth results from greater hope and increased exploration: Joining new and interesting groups, reading about and discussing ideas, considering different interests/hobbies/jobs, looking at educational pursuits, thinking about self-image and wherever that leads—new clothes or different haircuts, considering moves to different locations, joining exercise or traveling clubs/gyms. As suggested earlier, the client may select any or none of these ideas (or others) at her own pace.

Picking up the lost parts of self, creating new parts and then putting them together is like a puzzle, a puzzle enjoyed while in connection with

**Table 11.2. Susan's Coercive Abuse Climate Map
(Completed during therapy—see case story above)**

Type of Coercion	Coercive Tools	Demand	Response	Consequences, Feelings, Symptoms
Threats to kill me Drunk driving	Discounted me Threats Unsafe driving	Unsafe driving	Obeyed	1) Man killed 2) Horror, guilt 3) Sad, depressed Can't sleep Anxious Terrified

encouraging others; this is the transformation from confusion to clarification, from coercion to integration in connection.

Grief and Forgiveness

As noted earlier, coerced people experience grief and loss. They have lost a clear sense of identity. After coercion into illegal acts, the person can lose a job or career, even the respect of the larger community. Coercion involves betrayal and a loss of trust because the coercer is using the coerced for his own purposes without regard for her wishes or hopes, and sometimes exposing her to danger. Feelings of grief can occur after the injury or death of a pet or someone who has been harmed by the coercer's plot. Still, some coerced people miss the coercive person, whom they either once loved or still love.

Whether or not the coerced person fully realized the outcome of her specific, ordered actions, her self-blame can lead to depression, even thoughts about harming herself. It is important to listen for self-blame during therapy with the coerced, and the therapist should ask about the possibility of self-harm.

The coerced may move toward forgiving the coercer while disattaching from him and from the coercive process. Disattaching from the coercive process is hopefully a general learning experience, in order to avoid reattaching to this same or a similar process once again in the future. The most crucial part of the forgiving process is for her to forgive herself. This is an invitation, not a demand, from a forgiving therapist.

Steele views compassion toward the self as a goal in therapy (personal interview with Kathy Steele, February 9, 2015). This is valuable for the coerced who is in need of caring and compassion from herself and others.

Forgiveness is a process that does not happen all at once. Many of the coerced, eager to forgive themselves, discover a sense of peace and even meaning gained from the coercive experience. Some rely on a sense of faith for added strength. And new connections of the coerced often bring acceptance and even admiration for her skills and caring shared with others.

While self-forgiveness is challenging when many others express a lack of forgiveness, greater knowledge and understanding can lead to changes of attitudes in the community. There can be increased community acceptance toward a coerced person when more information about the coercion is shared (e.g., in trials and/or in the media) and when the coerced person organizes some form(s) of restitution, which many find helpful, even thrilling, for themselves and others. Great care must be taken in planning restitution, like the teenager described earlier who replaced flowers that had been pulled up and strewn about. Restitution plans should first be checked out with everyone from the victims to law enforcement, when appropriate.

However, in some situations, moving to another location may seem like a good option for the coerced. A new beginning can be a way of starting over when the lack of hope about community forgiveness seems realistic and lasting.

Discussion about the coercive abuse climate map can provide discovery for the coerced and a therapist. It is essential to view the full context of her behavior: Only then will self-forgiveness begin in the presence of a forgiving therapist. The goal is for her to hear and feel the therapist's understanding and clarification of what past and current forces drove her behavior. And the therapist grasps and understands terrifying pressures she faced: This is her road to recovery. The coerced is thrilled, first with the therapist's belief that she deserves compassion and forgiveness, and then with encouragement and permission from the therapist to be happy with wonderful experiences in life.

Nira's Lost Opportunity

Nira was living with her husband and three children in the United States. Nira's husband would not allow her to take their children to visit her father in Africa. Her husband had threatened to cause her deportation if she disobeyed his orders, adding that she would never see her children again if she was deported and they remained in America. In her culture in Africa, respect toward and consideration for elders held an important value, so Nira was disappointed in herself for failure to honor her cultural heritage.

Her husband hid the children's passports and birth certificates, which are needed for travel. And he isolated her from family members living in America. Nira went alone to visit her father in Africa. She was saddened when, after her return to America, her father died without having ever seen his teenage grandchildren. "I should have done something. I don't know what. I will never forgive myself for my father never meeting his grandkids."

Restoration of Hope

The coerced can feel a restored sense of hope as she emerges from guilt and regret. While she still feels sorrow about her behavior, hope is possible after therapeutic help with grief and forgiveness, clarification and growth of the self, and connecting with hopeful activities and/or people.

A therapeutic goal includes her seeking out people who share positive feedback about her efforts, personality, and journey in life. Connecting with heartfelt causes, she can, if she wishes, find hope in her accomplishments.

New experiences and connections open up possibilities for growth and development, again, if she wishes and at her own pace. More than from the therapist, alone, hope shines upon her from many directions.

For Nira, therapy helped in forgiving herself for not having taken her children to see their grandfather. Restoring a sense of hope led to her search for and discovery of the children's hidden passports. Money from her job had been saved in her bank account. After checking that she'd have no trouble reentering the country, she bought airplane tickets and took her children to see their grandmother in Africa. "I had to forgive myself that the children never met Daddy. But the chance for them to meet my mommy, that was a joy to me."

As part of her growing sense of hope and connection, the coerced may reach the point when group therapy would be helpful. It is important for the group leader to have knowledge about trauma, abuse, and coercion. Once she is more able to share herself, the woman may find support and additional clarification from other group members.

Transformation

Transformation occurs when the coerced is able to engage with the therapist to grieve about her own loss of self and resulting coerced behavior, to forgive herself for harm to others, and to allow herself hope for the future. When the therapist clarifies and supports grief and sadness for her losses and guilt, then a coerced woman is encouraged by example to understand, forgive herself, and embrace hope.

Conclusion

Everyone has values that are held dear. Most want to embrace (and be embraced by) loved ones with warmth, love, and loyalty. It is hard to imagine the shock of discovering that one bears some responsibility for hurt, pain, harm, or even death of a loved one—or someone else's loved one(s). And what must this be like for the coerced, who may have followed instructions from an intimate other, the very person who would be expected to support and encourage? Instead, the coercer has used unthinkable means of control, even threatening the death of a beloved pet, child, parent, or other loved one. The instructions may have seemed simple—buy this or that; drive the car; let me have alone time with my child. Who could imagine that the overall plan was to use what had been purchased to make a bomb, to demand driving for a bank robbery, to harm the child during alone time?

There is robbery of material things, but even more complex is the theft of another's integrated self, involving abuse that rivals Amnesty International's descriptions of coercion. It may be puzzling that this theft can befall even the brightest and most accomplished, who begin to whither on the inside like an unnourished plant, isolated from sunshine and water. The isolation, cruelty, and surveillance experienced by the coerced are sometimes hard to believe without documentation and witnesses, who may be all too few.

The key is context: As discussed by Loring and Beaudoin (2000), it is crucial to see a coerced person's behavior in the context of her experience rather than viewing it in isolation. Threats to harm pets, children, and other beloved ones are harsh and frightening to the coerced, especially

131

when there is evidence that the threats are real and likely to be carried out unless orders are obeyed. To live with that truth produces trauma, guilt, and self-blame—the choice is between two horrors: obedience or harm.

What a challenge, conveying this dilemma among the coerced! It is important to understand the struggles of a coerced person. How much of the end result did she recognize, while caught up with so much anxiety that spacing out became a way of life? And how far could she go in delaying or avoiding behaviors she was ordered to perform when those delays and avoidances put her own or others' lives at risk? The coerced's road to recovery is just that—a continual journey where, at any time and place, memories and feelings intrude about past terror, betrayed values, betrayal of love and caring, condemnation by others, loss of self-respect, and profound sadness. Most coerced people jump at the chance for restitution. Many do not have that opportunity.

The victims of coercive plots are often heartbroken with losses that are hard to imagine and rarely expected: Loss of money, harm or the death of loved ones, panic and trauma during robberies, plus other traumatic and life-changing experiences. For those trying to understand the coerced, these victims are a part of the suffering. Sharing compassion with them, whenever possible, can be important, both for their comfort and for any information they would like to provide for an evaluation.

It is crucial to recognize and help the children and adults (and animals) who are victims of coercion. And, even if the coercion does not involve illegal activities, the human cost and suffering is huge for anyone who is forced into behaviors that mock personal values, compelled to choose between obedience and sorrow, or haunted by medical problems symbolic of the broken-heartedness that results when one is coerced. For children, being coerced leaves an emptiness and distrust, a sense of being unimportant and only valued for their use to others, sometimes painful and demeaning sexual abuse. How can these children develop empathy toward others when they never experienced it themselves?

Humans are affected by and protective of each other—whether one is a teacher, relative, neighbor, therapist, health care provider, child protective worker, or church leader. Everyone must ask questions and cradle the information, trusting any perceptions or instincts that someone is in real trouble and needs help. Hopefully, the help occurs before one is caught up in the coercion of an illegal act and/or forced into behavior against deeply held values. Even while reaching out to help, we must be mindful of our own safety.

Whenever someone's behavior is viewed in the total context of their lives, a picture emerges that is multidimensional and real. Coercion is a powerful force and, when it operates as intimate coercion, the betrayal of caring and love is profound and sad. Yet intimate coercion can be challenging to recognize. Our hope is that this book will assist many to understand the dynamics and foundation of coercion, envision the impact of coercive experiences, view dynamics among the coerced and coercers, learn about different groups experiencing coercion, and understand interventions for recovery.

The authors extend their feelings of deep sorrow for victims whose lives have been changed forever by the coercers and the coerced.

Bibliography

Abramson, L. Y., Seligman, M. E. P., and Teasdale, J. D. (1978). "Learned Helplessness in Humans: Critique and Reformulation." *Journal of Abnormal Psychology* 87(1): 49–74.

American Psychiatric Association. (2013). *Diagnostic and Statistical Manual of Mental Disorders*, 5th edition, DSM-5. Washington, DC: American Psychiatric Publishing.

Ayyub, R. (2000). "Domestic Violence in the South Asian Muslim Immigrant Population in the United States." *Journal of Social Distress and the Homeless* 9: 237–48.

Beck, Judith S. (2011). *Cognitive Behavior Therapy*, 2nd ed. New York: Guilford.

Black, M. C., Basile, K. C., Breiding, M. J., Smith, S. G., Walters, M. L., Merrick, M. T., Chen, J., and Stevens, M. R. (2011). *The National Intimate Partner and Sexual Violence Survey (NISVS): 2010 Summary Report*. Atlanta, GA: National Center for Injury Prevention and Control, Centers for Disease Control and Prevention.

Biderman's Chart of Coercion. (1973). *Amnesty International, Report on Torture*. New York: Farrar, Straus, Giroux.

Coleridge, Samuel Taylor. (1950). *The Portable Coleridge*, edited by I. A. Richards. New York: Colonial Press, Inc.

Corrigan, Frank, and Grand, D. (2013). "Brainspotting: Recruiting the Midbrain for Accessing and Healing Sensorimotor." *Medical Hypotheses* 80(6): 759–66.

Craig, Gary. (1995). *The EFT Manual—Everyday EFT: Emotional Freedom Techniques*. Santa Rosa, CA: Energy Psychology Press.

Duke, A., and Davidson, M. (2009). "Same-Sex Intimate Partner Violence: Lesbian, Gay, and Bisexual Affirmative Outreach." *Journal of Aggression, Maltreatment and Trauma* 18: 795–816.

Dutton, D. G., and Painter, S. L. (1981). Traumatic Bonding: The Development of Emotional Bonds in Relationships of Intermittent Abuse. *Victimology: An International Journal* 6(1–4): 139–55.

Dutton, D. G., and Starzomski, A. J. (1997). "The Abusive Personality and the Minnesota Power and Control Wheel." *Journal of Interpersonal Violence* 12(1): 70–82.

Dutton, Donald. (1995). *The Batterer: A Psychological Profile*. New York: Basic Books.

Dutton, Donald, and Painter, Susan. (1993). "Emotional Attachments in Abusive Relationships: A Test of Traumatic Bonding Theory." *Violence and Victims* 8(2): 105–20.

Dutton, Mary Ann, and Goodman, Lisa. (2005). "Coercion in Intimate Partner Violence: Toward a New Conceptualization." *Sex Roles* 52(11/12): 743–59.

Dutton, Mary Ann, Goodman L., and Schmidt, R. J. (2006). *Development and Validation of a Coercive Control Measure for Intimate Partner Violence: Final Technical Report*. https://www.ncjrs.gov/pdffiles1/nij/grants/214438.pdf (accessed May 10, 2013).

Eliot. T. S. (1943, 2009). "Four Quartets." In *Selected Poems of T. S. Eliot* (p. 59). London: Faber and Faber.

Giordano, P., Soto, D., Manning, W., and Longmore, M. (2010). "The Characteristics of Romantic Relationships Associated with Teen Dating Violence." *Social Science Research* 39(6): 863–74.

Grand, D. (2013). *Brainspotting: The Revolutionary New Therapy for Rapid and Effective Change*. Boulder, CO: Sounds True.

Herman, Judith. (1997). *Trauma and Recovery: The Aftermath of Violence from Domestic Abuse to Political Terror*. Rev. 2nd ed. New York: Basic Books.

Hirigoyen, Marie-France. (2000). *Stalking the Soul: Emotional Abuse and the Erosion of Identity*. New York: Helen Marx Books.

Holzman, L. 2013. "'Vygotskian-izing' Psychotherapy." *Mind, Culture, and Activity* 21(3): 184–99.

Iverson, K., Shenk, C., and Fruzzetti, A. (2009). "Dialectical Behavior Therapy for Women Victims of Domestic Abuse: A Pilot Study." *Professional Psychology: Research and Practice* 40(3): 242–48.

Jones, Ann. 1994. *Next Time She'll Be Dead: Battering and How to Stop It*. Boston: Beacon Press.

Jordan, Judith. (2010). *Relational-Cultural Therapy*. Washington, DC: American Psychological Association.

Lempert, B. (1989). *L'enfant et le desamour*. Paris: Editions L'Arbre au milieu.

Levine, P. (1997). *Waking the Tiger: Healing Trauma*. Berkeley, CA: North Atlantic Books.

Linehan, M. M. (1993). *Cognitive Behavioral Treatment of Borderline Personality Disorder*. New York: Guilford Press.

Loring, Marti Tamm. (1994). *Emotional Abuse*. San Francisco: CA: Jossey-Bass.

Loring, Marti Tamm, and Beaudoin, P. (2000). "Battered Women as Coerced Victim-Perpetrators." *Journal of Emotional Abuse* 2(1): 3–14.

Loring, Marti, Geffner, R., and Marsh, J., eds. (2007). *Animal Abuse and Family Violence: Linkages, Research and Implications for Professional Practice*. New York: Haworth Maltreatment and Trauma Press.

Mayeroff, Milton. (1971). *On Caring*. New York: Harper and Row.

McGoldrick, M., Gerson R., and Shellenberger, S. (1999). *Genograms: Assessment and Intervention*, 2nd ed. New York: W.W. Norton.

Midlarsky, E., Venkataramani-Kothari, A., and Plante, M. (2006). "Domestic Violence in the Chinese and South Asian Immigrant Communities." *Annals of the New York Academy of Sciences* 1087: 279–300.

Millay, Edna St. Vincent. (1917). "My Heart, Being Hungry." In *Collected Lyrics of Edna St. Vincent Millay*. New York: Harper and Row.

Miller, Jean Baker. (1988). "Connections, Disconnections, and Violations." No. 33, Work in Progress Papers published by the Wellesley Centers for Women, Wellesley, MA.

Parker, C., Doctor, R., and Selvam, R. (2008). "Somatic Therapy Treatment: Effects with Tsunami Survivors." *Traumatology* 14(3): 103–9.

Partnoy, A. (1992). "Testimony." In *Revenge of the Apple* (p. 97). Pittsburgh, PA: Cleis.

Partnoy, A. (2014). "Por/traits." In *Fuegos Florales* (*Flowering Fires*) (p. 17), translated by Gail Wronsky. Silver Spring, MD: Settlement House.

Pence, E., and Paymar, M. (1986). *Power and Control: Tactics of Men Who Batter*. Duluth, MN: Minnesota Program Development, Inc

Pesso, Albert. (1973). *Experience in Action: A Psychomotor Psychology*. New York: New York University Press.

Pesso, Albert, and Boyden-Pesso, D. (2013). *Sharing the Practical Wisdom: A Compendium of PBSP: Concepts and Insights*, ed. by David Cooper. Amazon Kindle.

Richie, Beth. (1996). *Compelled to Crime: The Gender Entrapment of Battered Black Women*. New York: Routledge.

Sakheim, D. K., and Devine, S. E. (1992). "Bound by the Boundaries: Therapy Issues in Work with Individuals Exposed to Severe Trauma." In *Out of Darkness: Exploring Satanism and Ritual Abuse*, ed. Sakheim and Devine (pp. 279–93). Lexington, MA: Lexington Books.

Sexton, Anne. (1966). "Flee on Your Donkey." In *Live or Die*. Boston: Houghton Mifflin.

Shapiro, F. (1995). *Eye Movement Desensitization and Reprocessing: Basic Principles, Protocols and Procedures*. New York: Guilford Press.

Shapiro, F. (2013). *Getting Past Your Past: Take Control of Your Life with Self-Help Techniques from EMDR Therapy*. New York: Rodale Books.

Siegel, Ronald. (2010). *The Mindfulness Solution: Everyday Practices for Everyday Problems*. New York: Guilford Press.

Stark, Evan. (2007). *Coercive Control: How Men Entrap Women in Personal Life*. Oxford: Oxford University Press.

U.S. Department of Justice. (2013). *In Brief: Understanding Elder Abuse*. Washington, DC: Office of Justice Programs.

van der Kolk, Bessel. (1994). "The Body Keeps the Score: Memory and the Evolving Psychobiology of Post Traumatic Stress." *Harvard Review of Psychiatry* 1(5): 253–65.

van der Kolk, Bessel. (2014). *The Body Keeps Score: Brain, Mind and Body in the Healing of Trauma*. New York: Viking Penguin.

Vygotsky, Lev S. 1934. "The Problem of the Environment." In *The Vygotsky Reader*, ed. Rene van der Veer and Jaan Valsiner (pp. 338–54). Oxford: Wiley-Blackwell.

Walker, Lenore. (1984). *The Battered Woman Syndrome*. New York: Springer.

Warner, E., Spinazzola, J., Westcott, A., Gunn, C., and Hodgdon, H. (2014). "The Body Can Change the Score: Empirical Support for Somatic Regulation in the

Treatment of Traumatized Adolescents." *Journal of Child and Adolescent Trauma* 7(4): 237–46. link.springer.com/article/10.1007/s10896-013-9535-8 (accessed November 16, 2014).

Williamson, Marianne. (2002). *Everyday Grace: Having Hope, Finding Forgiveness, and Making Miracles*. New York: Riverhead Books.

Yucha, C., and Montgomery, D. (2008). *Evidence-Based Practice in Biofeedback and Neurofeedback*. Wheat Ridge, CO: Association for Applied Psychophysiology.

Index

abandonment: fear of, 27–29, 53; threats of, 83, 106

abuse, xx; in adolescents, 99; coercion and, xvi, 22–26; culture and, 93; hidden and denied, 35–36; pet/animal, 88; questions for uncovering, 63–64; as way of life, 55. *See also specific types of abuse*

abused: connection and, 113; emotional regulation in, 17–18; therapeutic practices for, 8–17; treatment of, 7–19

adolescents, xiv; abuse among, 99. *See also* teen coercion

affirmations, 10

alcohol abuse, xviii, 89; history of, 75; self-medicating with, 61

amnesia, 34. *See also* dissociation

anger, in coercer, 48

anxiety, 37

arrest: of coerced, 75; coercion after, 115; relief after, of coerced, 81

authority, church coercion and, 107–8

Baker Miller, Jean, 30, 57

bank robbery, coercion in, 79–80

battered women: citizenship status of immigrant, 94; DBT for, 15–16; illegal behavior and, 4; staying with abusive partner, 52–55

batterers: coercers as, 48–49; types and purposes of, 47–48

Beck, Aaron, 14–15

behavior, xv–xvi; context of, 3; uncharacteristic, xviii; unusual, xviii; values and, xviii; violent, xviii

belief: core, 15; in harm, 27–29

Biderman's Chart of Coercion, 2; correct perception in, 107–8; debility and exhaustion in, 40–41; devaluing individual in, 41; isolation in, 40; rare praise in, 108

biofeedback, neurofeedback and, 12–13

bisexuals, 96

Boon, Suzette, 8

Brainspotting, 13–14

brainwashing, 40–41

Buford, Paula, 8

CAPS. *See* Clinician-Administered PTSD Scale

captivity: cage of coercive control, 1; of coerced, 39–40, 57–58
caregivers, elder abuse and, 102
caring, process of, 113
CBT. *See* cognitive behavior therapy
change: agents, transformation of coerced and, 115; in coercer, 50–51
childhood abuse, 51
children, xiv; coercion toward, 109–12, 132; harm to, 23–24
church partners, coercion of, 107–9; psychosocial evaluation of, 108–9
citizenship status of battered immigrants, 94
clarification, relational connective intervention, 124–28; Coercive Abuse Climate Map, 125–26, *126*; process of, 123
Clinician-Administered PTSD Scale (CAPS), 66
co-dependency, 115; mislabeling of, xix
coerced, xii, 37–44; arrest of, 75; captivity of, 39–40, 57–58; complex issues among, 87; cooperation of, 76; emotional regulation in, 17–18; health problems of, 43–44, 87; helplessness and, 38; illegal behavior by, 5–6, 40; individual therapy for, 114; recovery of, 132; relief after arrest of, 81; separation from coercer, 43–44; staying with coercer, 52–55; therapeutic intervention with, 19, 119–30; torture and brainwashing of, 40–41; transformation of, xvi–xvii, 46, 113–17; trauma among, 37–39, 113; traumatic bonding and, 41–43; trauma victims and, 113; view of, xviii; wholeness of self, 116
coerced behavior: context of, 3, 25, 131–32; illegal, xvi, xxi, 22–26, 49–50, 67–68
coercer, xii; abuse as way of life for, 55; anger in, 48; as batterer, 48–49; change in, 50–51; coerced's separation from, 43–44; coerced

staying with, 52–55; emotionally abusive, as consultants, 50–51; interviewing, 45–46; justifications, 49–50; as person of power, 39; in relationships, 45–55; stalking by, 52; in therapy, 47; unrelated charges faced by, 51–52; vulnerabilities exploited by, 28
coercion: abuse and, xvi, 22–26; after arrest, 115; in bank robbery, 79–80; distal, 32–33; drug abuse and, 22; Dutton and Goodman's framework of, 3; effects of, xix; emotional abuse and, 25–26; evaluation of, 63–90; factors, 3–4; financial, 102; in financial fraud, 82–83; genograms about, 89–90; identifying, 63–64; in other groups, 93–112; physical abuse and, 22–24; in power and control wheel, 1–2; remnants of, 114–15; sexual abuse and, 24–25; women and, xvi–xviii
Coercive Abuse Climate Map, 125–26, *126, 127*; self-forgiveness and, 129
coercive control: cage of, 1; nonviolent, 4; Stark's model of, 2–3; violent, 2
Coercive Control (Stark), 2
coercive map, 126
coercive process, 57–61, 119
cognitive behavior therapy (CBT), 14–15
collateral witnesses, xiii, 65, 68–69; in psychosocial evaluation, 71–72; relationship history and, 78–79
community: forgiveness and, 128–29; South Asian community, physical abuse in, 93–94
compassion, toward self, 128
Compelled to Crime (Ritchie), 4
complex issues, among coerced, 87
complex PTSD, 8
compliance, 40–41
confidentiality, evaluation of coercion and, 70–71
connection: abused and, 113; for traumatized, 113–14

Rasche, Carolyn, 11
rebuilding self, relational connective
intervention, 124
recognizing intimate coercion, 21–26,
132; threats and harm, 21
recommendation section, psychosocial
evaluation, 86
recovery, of coerced, 132
relational connective intervention,
eight components of: clarification,
124–28; grief and forgiveness, 128–
29; rebuilding self, 124; restoration
of hope, 129–30; therapeutic
endeavor, 122–23; therapeutic
mode, 123–24; therapeutic stance,
120–22; transformation, 130
relational encouragement, 121
relationships, coercer in, 45–55.
See also history of relationships,
psychosocial evaluation
release forms, 68, 70
restitution, 128–29, 132
restoration of hope, relational
connective intervention, 129–30
Ritchie, Beth: *Compelled to Crime*, 4;
gender-entrapment theoretical
model, 4–5
ritualized emotional abuse, 31–32, 117

safety, 54, 127
same-sex abuse, 96. *See also* gay
couples
Scardaville, Melissa, xv–xvi
Schmidt, R. James, 4
Schwartzberg, Cynthia, 13
self: coercion and, xvi; compassion
toward, 128; dissolution, 29–30;
intimate partner violence and sense
of, 5; rebuilding, 124; separation of,
115; wholeness of, coerced's, 116
self-blame, 128
self-esteem, 43, 54
self-forgiveness, 128–29
self-harm, 36, 128; covert emotional
abuse and, 61
self-medicating, 61

sensory motor arousal regulation
treatment (SMART), 18
separation: of coerced from coercer,
43–44; of self, 115
sexual abuse, coercion and, 24–25
sexual coercion, intimate partner
violence and, 6
sexual orientation, threats to expose,
96
sexual violence, 6
Shapiro, Francine, 10–11; *Getting Past
Your Past: Take Control of Your
Life with Self- Help Techniques from
EMDR Therapy*, 10
siblings, coercion toward children by,
110
Siegel, Ronald, 9
SMART. *See* sensory motor arousal
regulation treatment
social therapy, 16
Somatic Experiencing Therapy, 14
South Asian community, physical
abuse in, 93–94
stalking: as coercive tactic, 52; intimate
partner violence and, 6
Stark, Evan, 1, 26; *Coercive Control*,
2; model of coercive control, 2–3;
opposition to subjugation described
by, 27; surveillance, 31
staying with abusive partner, 52–55
Steele, Kathy, 8, 114
Stockholm Syndrome, 5; traumatic
bonding and, 42
subjugation, opposition to, 27
suicidal ideation, 61
surveillance, 4, 31

tapping in, 9–10
teen coercion, 99–102; diagnosis of,
101; psychosocial evaluation of,
100–101
teen violence programs, 102
testifying, 94
theater, 16–17
therapeutic endeavor, relational
connective intervention, 122–23

Lightning Source UK Ltd.
Milton Keynes UK
UKOW02n2308150716

278461UK00009B/138/P